T. DE WITT TALMAGE

Selected and Edited by

MAY TALMAGE

BAKER BOOK HOUSE
Grand Rapids, Michigan 49506

Originally published in 1922 by
George H. Doran Company
under the title,
The Wisdom and Wit of T. De Witt Talmage

Reprinted 1968 by Baker Book House
under the title,
The Treasury of T. De Witt Talmage

Mass market paperback edition
issued 1982 by Baker Book House

ISBN: 0-8010-8863-1

PHOTOLITHOPRINTED BY CUSHING - MALLOY, INC.
ANN ARBOR, MICHIGAN, UNITED STATES OF AMERICA

FOREWORD

These selections were made by me from the writings of my father whose sermons were published every Monday morning in all the large cities, and many of the small towns in America, England, Ireland, Scotland, Australia, and New Zealand, and translated into foreign languages. His was an every-day religion, full of sunshine, flowers, music, health, hope, encouragement. His principal theme was Heaven, and his messages have not grown old or stale with the passing years.

MAY TALMAGE.

CONTENTS

AGE

AMUSEMENTS

BOOKS

BIBLE

CHARACTER

CHARACTER (*Continued*)

CHEERFULNESS

CHILDREN

CHRIST

CHURCH

CONTENTS

CHURCH (*Continued*)

COMPANIONSHIP

COMPENSATION

CONCUSSION

CONSOLATION

CROAKERS

DETERMINATION

DISSIPATION

DIVINE SATIRE

ENCOURAGEMENT

FIDELITY

FLOWERS

FORGIVENESS

FRIENDSHIP

GOD

HAPPINESS

CONTENTS

HEALTH

HEAVEN

HOME

INDIVIDUALS AS FRAGMENTS

INDOLENCE

INFLUENCE

INSIGNIFICANCES

INTEMPERANCE

KINDNESS

LIES

LIFE

CONTENTS

MAN

MASTER OF THE SITUATION

MOTHER

MUSIC

NAME

NON-APPRECIATION

OPPORTUNITY

CONTENTS

REMINISCENCE

THE SEASONS

SERVICE

SILENCE

SNOW

SONGS

STARS

TIME

TIME (*Continued*)

TROUBLE

UPPER FORCES

WOMAN

WORLD

T. DE WITT TALMAGE

Life, Like Fruit, Should Grow Mellow.—Horatio Greenough, at the close of the hardest life a man ever lived—the life of an American artist—wrote: "I don't want to leave this world until I give some sign that, born by the grace of God in this land, I have found life to be a very cheerful thing, and not the dark and bitter thing with which my early prospects were clouded." Albert Barnes, the good Christian, known the world over, stood in his pulpit in Philadelphia, at seventy or eighty years of age, and said: "This world is so very attractive to me, I am very sorry I shall have to leave it." I know that Solomon said some very dolorous things about this world, and three times declared: "Vanity of vanities, all is vanity." Yet I do not think that Solomon was there declaring a doctrine. I think he was giving his own personal experience. I suppose his seven hundred wives almost pestered the life out of him. I would rather turn to the description he gave after his conversion when he says in another place: "Her ways are ways of pleasantness, and all her paths are peace." It is reasonable to expect life will be so. The longer the fruit hangs on the tree, the riper and more mellow it ought to grow.

Happiness Increases with Age.—I correct the popular impression that people are happier in childhood and youth than they ever will be again. If we live aright; the older, the happier. The happiest woman that I ever knew was a Christian octogenarian; her hair white as white could be; the sunlight of heaven late in the afternoon gilding the peaks of snow. As you advance in life, as you come out into the world and have your head and heart full of good, honest, practical Christian work, then you will know what it is to begin to be happy.

Time Represented with a Scythe.—Longevity never cures impenitency. All the pictures of Time represent him with a scythe to cut, but I never saw any picture of Time with a case of medicines to heal. Seneca says that Nero for the first five years of his public life, was set up as an example of clemency and kindness, but his path all the way descended until at sixty-eight years he became a suicide. If eight hundred years did not make antediluvians any better, but only made them worse, the ages of eternity could have no effect, except prolongation of depravity.

Beauty of Old Age.—If there is anything on earth beautiful to me it is an aged woman, her white locks flowing back over the wrinkled brow—locks not white with frost, as the poets say, but white with the blossoms of the tree of life, in her voice the tenderness of gracious memories, her face a benediction. As grandmother passes through the room her grandchildren pull at her dress, and she almost falls in her weakness. When she goes away from us never to return, there is a shadow on the table and a shadow on the hearth and a shadow on the heart. Oh, there is a beauty in old age. God says so. "The hoary head is a crown of glory."

Caricature of Age.—Why should people be sorry to get old? The best things, the greatest things I know of, are aged. But if there is anything distressful, it is to see an old woman ashamed of the fact that she is old. What with all the artificial appliances, she is too much for my gravity. I laugh even in church, when I see her coming. The worst-looking bird on earth is a peacock when it has lost its feathers. I would not give one lock of my old mother's gray hair for a thousand such caricatures of humanity.

Glorious Old Age.—Glorious old age, if found in the way of righteousness! How beautiful the old age of Jacob, leaning on the top of his staff; of John Quincy Adams, falling with the harness on; of Washington Irving, sitting, pen in hand, amid the scenes himself had made classical. See that you do honor to the aged. A philosopher stood at the corner of the street day after day saying to the passers-by, "You will be an old man; you will be an old woman." People thought that he was crazy. I do not think that he was.

Talleyrand.—On Bowling Green, New York, there is a house where Talleyrand used to go. He was a favored man. All the world knew him, and he had wealth almost unlimited; yet at the close of his life he says, "Behold, eighty-three years have passed without any practical result save fatigue of mind, great discouragement for the future, and great disgust for the past."

AMUSEMENTS

"Rejoice Evermore!"—Our communities are filled with men and women who have in their souls unmeasured resources for sportfulness and frolic. Show me the man who never lights up with sportfulness, and has no sympathy with the recreation of others, and I will show you a man who is a stumbling block. Such men are caricatures of religion. They lead young people to think that a man is good in proportion as he groans, and frowns, and looks sallow; and that the height of a man's Christian stature is in proportion to the length of his face. I would trade off five hundred such men for one bright-faced radiant Christian, on whose face are the words, "Rejoice evermore!" I will go further and say that I have no confidence in a man who makes a religion of his gloomy looks. That kind of man always turns out badly. I would not want him for the treasurer of an orphan asylum. The orphans would suffer.

Our religion is a bright angel, feet bright, eyes bright, wings bright, taking her place in the soul. Go forth, O people, to your lawful amusements. God means you to be happy. But when there are so many sources of innocent pleasures why tamper with anything that is dangerous and polluting? Why stop our ears to a heaven full of songsters, to listen to the hiss of a dragon? Why turn your back from the mountainside all abloom with wild flowers and a-dash with the nimble torrents, and with blistered feet attempt to climb the sides of Cotopaxi?

Religion of "Don'ts."—For the last hundred years the Church has spent much of its time in denouncing hurtful and dangerous amusements—a cautionary work most important and necessary; but it seems to me that we have stopped short of the mark. Having been so long in telling the people what they must not do, it seems to me about time to tell them what they may do. This world will never be reformed by a religion of "don'ts." There is an unlawful use of amusement but the difference between the man Christian and the man un-Christian is that the former masters the world, while in the latter case the world masters him.

The Reaction of Amusements.—Amusement has either healthful result or baneful reaction. There are people who seem made up of hard facts. They are a combination of multiplication tables and statistics. If you show them an exquisite picture they will begin to discuss the pigments involved in the coloring; if you show them a beautiful rose, they will submit it to a botanical analysis, which is only the post-mortem examination of the flower. They never do anything more than feebly smile. There are no great tides of feeling surging up from the depth of their soul in billow after billow of reverberating laughter. They seem as if nature had built them by contract and made a bungling job out of it. But blessed be God, there are people in the world who have bright faces and whose life is a song, an anthem, a pean of victory. Even their troubles are like the vines that crawl up the side of a great tower, on the top of which the sunlight sits and the soft airs of summer hold perpetual carnival. They are the people you like to have come to your house; they are the people I like to come to my house. Now, it is these exhilarant and sympathetic and warm-hearted people that are most tempted to pernicious amusements. In proportion as a ship is swift it wants a strong helmsman; in proportion as a horse is spirited, it wants a strong driver; and these people of exuberant nature will do well to look at the reaction of all their amusements.

Healthful Recreations.—You may judge of amusements by their effects upon physical health. The need of many good people is physical recuperation. God will hold you responsible for your invalidism if it is your own fault, and when through right exercise and prudence you might be well and athletic. There are great hearts and intellects in bodies worn out by their own neglects. Magnificent machinery capable of propelling a great liner across the Atlantic, yet fastened in a rickety North River propeller. A man may through some of the popular and healthful recreations of our time work off his spleen and his querulousness and one half of his physical and mental ailments.

An Investment.—Money spent in recreation is not thrown away. It is folly for us to come from a place of amusement feeling that we have wasted our time and money. You may by it have made an investment worth more than the transaction that yielded thousands of dollars. But how many properties have been riddled by costly amusements? The table has been robbed to pay the club dues. The champagne has cheated the children's wardrobe. The carousing party has burned up the boy's primer. Excursions that in a day make a tour around a whole month's wages. Women whose lifetime habit it is to "go shopping" have their counterpart in uneducated children in bankruptcies that shock the money market and appall the church. When men go into amusements that they cannot afford, they first borrow what they cannot earn, and then they steal what they cannot borrow. They go into embarrassment and then into theft; and when a man gets as far as that he does not stop short of the penitentiary. There is not a prison in the land where there are not victims of unsanctified amusements.

BOOKS

The Power of a Book.—A good book—who can estimate its power? Benjamin Franklin said that his reading of Cotton Mather's "Essays to Do

Good" in childhood gave him holy aspirations for all the rest of his life. Oh, the power of a good book! But, alas! for the influence of a bad book.

We see so many books, we do not understand what a book is. Stand it on end. Measure it, the height of it, the depth of it, the length of it, the breadth of it. You cannot do it. Examine the paper and estimate the progress made from the time of the impressions on clay and then on to the bark of trees, and from the bark of trees to papyrus, and from papyrus to the hide of wild beasts, and from the hide of wild beasts on down until the miracles of our modern paper manufactories, and then see the paper white, pure as an infant's soul, waiting for God's inscription. A book! Examine the type of it. Examine the printing of it and see the progress from the time when Solon's laws were written on oak plans, and Hesiod's poems were written on tables of lead, and the Sinaitic were written on tables of stone, on down to Hoe's perfecting printing-press. It took all the universities of the past, all the martyr fires, all the civilizations, all the battles, all the victories, all the defeats, all the glooms, all the brightness, all the centuries to make it possible. A book! It is the chorus of the ages—it is the drawing room in which kings and queens and orators and poets, and historians and philosophers come out to greet you. If I worshiped anything on earth I would worship that. If I burned any incense to any idol I would build an altar to that. Thank God for good books, healthful books, inspiring books, Christian books, books for men, books for women, Book of God. It is with these good books that we are to overcome corrupt literature.

The Art Not to Read.—It is as much an art not to read as it is to read. With what pains and thumps and whacks at school we first learned the way to put words together! We did not mind so much being whipped by the schoolmaster for not knowing how to read our lessons, but to have to go out ourselves and cut the hickory switch with which the chastisement was to be inflicted seemed to us then as now a great injustice.

Notwithstanding all our hard work in learning to read, we find it quite hard now to learn how not to read. In this day readers need as never before to carry a sieve. It requires some heroism to say you have not read such and such a book. Your friend gives you a stare which implies your literary inferiority. Do not in order to answer the question affirmatively wade through indiscriminate slush. We have to say that three-fourths of the novels of the day are mental depletion to those who read them. The man who makes wholesale denunciation of fiction pitches overboard "Pilgrim's Progress" and the parables of our Lord. But the fact is that some of the publishing houses that once were cautious about the moral tone of their books have become reckless about everything but the number of copies sold.

Whether young or old be cautious about what you read in the newspapers. You cannot day by day go through three columns of murder trials without being a worse man than when you began. Skip that half page of divorce case. Keep out of the mud. With so much healthful literature of all sorts there is no excuse for bringing your minds in contact with evil. If there were a famine there might be some reason for eating garbage, but the land is full of bread. When we may with our families sit around the clean warm fire-hearth of Christian knowledge, why go hunting in the ash barrels for cinders.

The Plague of Corrupt Literature.—The plague of corrupt literature has taken, at different times, possession of this country. It is one of the most loathsome, one of the most frightful, one of the most ghastly of the plagues of modern cities. There is a vast number of books and newspapers printed which ought never to see the light. They are filled with a pestilence that makes the land swelter with a moral epidemic. The literature of a nation decides the fate of a nation. Good books, good morals. Bad books, bad morals.

Drive back this plague of corrupt literature by filling the minds of our boys and girls with healthful literature.

I do not mean that all the books and newspapers in our families ought to be religious books and newspapers, or that every song ought to be sung to the tune of "Old Hundred." I have no sympathy with the attempt to make the young old. I would rather join in a crusade to keep the young young. Boyhood and girlhood must not be abbreviated. But there are good books, good histories, good biographies, good works of fiction, good books of all styles with which we are to fill the minds of the young, so that there will be no more room for the useless and the vicious than there is room for chaff in a bushel measure which is already filled with Michigan wheat.

"Oh," says some one, "I am a business man, and I have no time to examine what my children read. I have no time to inspect the books that come into my household." If your children were threatened with typhoid fever, would you have time to go for the doctor? Would you have time to watch the progress of the disease? Would you have time for the funeral? In the presence of God I warn you of the fact that your children are threatened with moral and spiritual typhoid, and that unless the thing be stopped, it will be to them a funeral of body, funeral of mind, funeral of soul. Three funerals in one day.

Some Enigmas Solved.—There are passages of Scripture that once were enigmas, puzzles, riddles, and impossible for you to understand; you said, "I do not see why David keeps rolling over in his Psalms the story of how he was pursued and persecuted." He describes himself as surrounded by bees; he says, "They compassed me about like bees; yea, they compassed me about like bees." You think what an exaggerated thing for him to exclaim: "Out of the depths of hell have I cried unto thee, O Lord," and there is so much of that kind of lamentation in his writings you think he overdoes it, but after a while persecution comes upon you and you are pierced with this censure and wounded with defamation and stung with some falsehood, and lies in swarms are buzzing, buzzing about your ears, and at last you understand what David meant when he said: "They compassed me about like bees, yea, they compassed me about like bees," and you go down under nervous prostration and feel that you are down as far as David when he cried, "Out of the depth of hell."

Put down all the promises of the Bible on a table for study and put on one side of the table a man who has never had any trouble or very little of it and pile upon the table beside him all the encyclopedias, and all dictionaries, and all archeologies, and all commentaries; and on the other side of the table put a man who has had trial after trial, disaster upon disaster and let him begin the study of the promises without the lexicon, without commentary, without any book to explain or help and this latter man will understand far more the height and depth and length and breadth of these promises than the learned exegete opposite almost submerged in sacred literature.

A Versatile Book.—The Bible is the strangest, the loveliest, the mightiest, the weirdest, the best of books. Written by Moses the lawyer, Joshua the soldier, Samuel the judge, Ezra the scholar, Nehemiah the builder, Job the poet, David the shepherd, Daniel the prime minister, Amos the herdsman, Matthew the customhouse officer, Luke the doctor, Paul the missionary, John the exile; and yet a complete harmony from the middle verse of the Bible—which is the eighth verse of the one hundred and eighteenth Psalm —shortest passage— which is the thirty-fifth verse of the eleventh chapter of John—to the longest verse—which is the ninth verse of the eighth chapter of Esther—and yet not an imperfection in all the seven hundred and seventy-three thousand, six hundred and ninety-three words which it is composed of. It not only reaches over the past, but over the future, has in it a ferry-boat, as in second Samuel; and a telegraphic wire, as in Job; and a railroad train as in Nahum; and introduces us to a foundryman by the name of Tubal Cain, and a shipbuilder by the name of Noah, and an architect by the name of Aholiab, and tells us how many stables Solomon had to take care of his horses, and how much he paid for those horses. But few things in this versatile and comprehensive book interest me so much as its apothegms—those short, terse, sententious, epigrammatic sayings.

Bible Presents All Types of Character.—There is a great variety in the Scriptural landscape. God in his Word sets before us the beauty of self-denial, of sobriety, of devotion, of courage, and then, lest we should not thoroughly understand him, he introduced Daniel and Paul and Deborah as illustrations of those virtues. God also speaks to us in his Word as to the hatefulness of pride, of folly, of impiety, and lest we should not thoroughly understand him, introduces Nebuchadnezzar as the impersonation of these forms of depravity. The former style of character is a lighthouse, showing us a way into a safe harbor, and the latter style of character is a black buoy, swinging on the rocks to show where vessels wreck themselves.

Belief in the Bible.—Do not jump overboard from the staunch old-fashioned orthodoxy until there is something ready to take you up stronger than the fantastic yawl which has painted on the side "Advanced Thought" and which leaks at the prow and leaks at the stern and has a steel pen for one oar and a glib tongue for the other oar, and now tips over this way and then tips over that way, until you do not know whether the passengers will land in the breakers of despair, or on the sinking sands of infidelity and atheism.

I am in full sympathy with the advancements of our time, but this world will never advance a single inch beyond the old Bible. God was just as capable of dictating the truth to the prophets and apostles as He is capable of dictating the truths to these modern apostles and prophets. God has not learned anything in a thousand years. He knew just as much when He gave the first dictation as He does now, giving the last dictation, if He is giving any dictation at all. So I stick to the old paths. Naturally a skeptic, and preferring new things to old, I never so much as now felt the truth in the entire Bible. I prefer the thick warm robe which has kept so many warm amid the cold pilgrimage of this life and amid the chills of death. The old robe rather than the thin, uncertain gauze offered us by these wiseacres who believe the Bible in spots.

Consolatory Bible.—For a long time the Bible seemed lop-sided and a disproportionate amount of it given up to the consolatory. Why page after page and chapter after chapter and book after book in the Bible taken up with alleviations, with pacifications, with condolence? The book seems like an apothecary store with one-half of the shelves occupied with balsams. Why such a superfluity of balsams? But after awhile the membranous croup carries off your child, or your health gives way under the grip, or your property is swept off by a bad investment, or perhaps all three troubles come at once, bankruptcy, sickness and bereavement. Now the consolatory parts of Bible do not seem to be so disproportionate. You want something off almost all the shelves of the sacred dispensary.

Mild doses of medicine will do for mild sickness, but violent pains need strong doses and so I stand over you and count out some drops that will alleviate your worst troubles if you will only take the medicine, and here it is, "In the world ye shall have tribulations, but be of good cheer; I have overcome the world." "Weeping may endure for a night, but joy cometh in the morning."

A Transparent Bible.—It is a transparent Bible. All the mountains of the Bible come out; Sinai, the mountain of the law; Pisgah, the mountain of prospect; Olivet, the mountain of instruction; Calvary, the mountain of sacrifice. All the rivers of the Bible come out: Hidekel, or the river of paradisaical beauty; Jordan, or the river of holy chrism; Cherith, or the river of prophetic supply; Nile, or the river of palaces; and the pure river of life from under the throne, clear as crystal. While reading this Bible after our eyes have been touched by grace, we find it all transparent, and the earth rocks, now with crucifixion agony and now with judgment terror, and Christ appears in some of his two hundred and fifty-six titles, as far as I can count them—the bread, the rock, the captain, the commander, the conqueror, the star, and on beyond any capacity of mine to rehearse. Transparent religion!

The Ornithology of the Bible.—The ornithology of the Bible is a very interesting study. The stork which knoweth her appointed time. The common sparrows teaching the lesson of God's providence. The ostriches of the desert, by careless incubation, illustrating the recklessness of parents who do not take enough pains with their children. The eagle symbolizing riches which take wings and fly away. The pelican emblemizing solitude. The bat, a flake of the darkness. The night hawk, the ossifrage, the cuckoo, the lapwing, the osprey, by the command of God in Leviticus, flung out of the world's bill of fare.

I would like to have been with Audubon as he went through the woods, with gun and pencil, bringing down and sketching the fowls of heaven, his unfolded portfolio thrilling all Christendom. What wonderful creatures of God birds are! Some of them, this morning, like the songs of heaven let loose, bursting through the gates of heaven. Consider their feathers, which are clothing and conveyance at the same time; the nine vertebræ of the neck, the three eyelids to each eye, the third eyelid an extra curtain for graduating the light of the sun. Some of these birds scavengers and some of them orchestra. Thank God for quail's whistle and lark's carol and the twittering of the wren, called by the ancients the king of birds, because when the fowls of heaven went into a contest as to who could fly the highest, and the eagle swung nearest the sun, a wren on the back of the eagle, after the eagle was exhausted sprang up much higher and so was called by the ancients the king of birds. Consider those of them that have golden crowns and crests, showing them to be feathered imperials. And listen to the humming-bird's serenade in the ear of the honey-suckle. Look at the belted kingfisher, striking like a dart from sky to water. Listen to the voice of the owl, giving the keynote to all croakers. And behold the condor among the Andes, battling with the fallow-deer. I do not know whether an aquarium or aviary is the best altar from which to worship God.

The Bible a Parental Letter.—The Bible is a warm letter of affection from a parent to a child, and yet there are many who see chiefly the severer passages. As there may be fifty or sixty nights of gentle dew in one summer that will not cause as much remark as one hail-storm of half hour, so there are those who are more struck by those passages of the Bible that utter the indignation of God than by those that express his affection. There may come to a household twenty or fifty letters of affection during the year, and they will not make as much excitement in that home as one sheriff's writ; and so there are people who are more attentive to those passages which declare the wrath of God than to those which assure his mercy and his favor.

Scientific Opposition to Bible Overcome.—When science began to make its brilliant discoveries there were great facts brought to light that seemed to overthrow the truth of the Bible. The archæologist with his crowbar and the geologist with his hammer and the chemist with his batteries charged upon the Bible. Moses' account of the creation seemed disproved by the very structure of the earth. The astronomer wheeled round his telescope until the heavenly bodies seemed to marshal themselves against the Bible, as the stars in their courses fought against Sisera. Observatories and universities rejoiced at what they considered the extinction of Christianity. They gathered new courage at what they considered past victory, and pressed on their conquest into the kingdom of nature until, alas for them! they discovered too much. God's word had only been lying in ambush, that in some unguarded moment, with a sudden bound, it might tear infidelity to pieces. The discoveries of science seemed to give temporary victory against God and the Bible, and for a while the church acted as if she were on a retreat; but when all the opposers of God and truth had joined in the pursuit, and were sure of the field, Christ gave the signal to his church and, turning, they drove back their forces in shame. There was found to be no antagonism between nature and Revelation. The universe and the Bible were found to be the work of the same hand, two strokes of the same pen and their authorship the same God.

Decipher the Hieroglyphics.—When the French army went down into Egypt under Napoleon, an engineer, in digging for a fortress, came across a tablet which had been called the Rosetta stone. There were inscriptions in three or four languages on that Rosetta stone. Scholars studying out the alphabet of hieroglyphics from that stone were enabled to read ancient inscriptions on monuments and on tombstones. Well, many of the handwritings of God in our life are indecipherable hieroglyphics; we cannot understand them until we take up the Rosetta stone of divine inspiration, and the explanation all comes out, and the mysteries all vanish, and what was before beyond our understanding now is plain in its meaning, as we read, "All things work together for good to those who love God." So we decipher the hieroglyphics.

CHARACTER

Character of Soul in the Face.—The character of the face is decided by the character of the soul. The main features of our countenance were decided by the Almighty, and we cannot change them; but under God we decide whether we shall have countenances benignant or baleful, sour or sweet, wrathful or genial, benevolent or mean, honest or scoundrelly, impudent or modest, courageous or cowardly, frank or sneaking. In all the works of God there is nothing more wonderful than the human countenance. Though the longest face is less than twelve inches from hair line of the forehead to the bottom of the chin, and the broadest face is less than eight inches from cheek bone to cheek bone, yet in that small compass God hath wrought such differences that the sixteen hundred million of the human race may be distinguished from each other by their facial appearances. The face is ordinarily the index of character. It is the throne of emotions. It is the battlefield of the passions. It is the catalogue of character. It is the map of the mind. It is the geography of the soul. And while the Lord decides before our birth whether we shall be handsome or homely, we are, by the character we form, deciding whether our countenances shall be pleasant or disagreeable. This is so much so that some of the most beautiful faces are unattractive, because of their arrogance or their deceitfulness, and some of the most rugged and irregular features are attractive because of the kindness that shines through them. Accident, or sickness, or scarification may veil the face so that it shall not express the soul, but in the majority of cases give me a deliberate look at a man's countenance and I will tell you whether he is a cynic or an optimist, whether he is a miser or a philanthropist, whether he is noble or dastardly, whether he is good or bad.

Character Away from Home.—My subject impresses me with the beauty of youthful character remaining incorrupt away from home. If Daniel had plunged into every wickedness of the city of Babylon, the old folks at home would never have heard of it. If he had gone through all the rounds of iniquity, it would have cast no shadow on his early home. There were no telegraphs, there were no railroads. But Daniel knew that God's eye was on him. That was enough. There are young men not so good away from home as at home. Frederick tending his father's sheep among the hills, or threshing rye in the barn, is different perhaps from Frederick on the Stock Exchange. Instead of the retiring disposition, there is bold effrontery; instead of an obliging spirit, there is perhaps oppressive selfishness; instead of open-handed charity, there is tight-fisted stinginess; instead of reasonable hours, there is midnight revel. I speak to many young men on this matter. You who may have left your father's house, and others who though still under the parental roof, are looking forward to the time when you will go forth to conflict, alone in the world, with its temptations and its sorrows and when you will build up your own character. Oh, that the God of Daniel might be with you in Babylon!

Immediate Advice.—Zechariah, of my text, was a young man and in a day-dream he saw and heard two angels talking about the rebuilding of the city of Jerusalem. One of these angels desires that young Zechariah should be well informed about the rebuilding of that city, its circumference and the height of its walls, and he says to the other angel, "Run, speak to this young man." Do not walk, but run, for the message is urgent and imminent. So every young man needs to have immediate advice about the dimensions, the height and the circumference of that which under God he is to build, namely, his own character and destiny. No slow or laggard pace will do. A little further on, and counsel will be of no advantage. Swift-footed must be the practical and important suggestions, or they might as well never be made at all. Run at the pace of seven miles the hour, and speak to that young man. Run, before this year is ended. Run, before this century is closed. Run, before his character is inexorably decided for two worlds, this world and the next. How many of us have found out by long and bitter experience things that we ought to have been told before we were twenty-five years of age.

Good and Genial Character Requisite in Marriage. —Good and genial character in a man is the very first requisite for a woman's happy marriage. There is a tragedy repeated every hour of every day, all over Christendom—marriage of worldly success, without regard to character. So Marie Jeanne Philipon, the daughter of the humble engraver, became the famous Madame Roland of history, the vivacious and brilliant girl, united with the cold, formal, monotonous man, because he came of an affluent family of Amiens, and had lordly blood in his veins. The day when, through political revolution, this patriotic woman was led to the scaffold, around which lay piles of human heads that had fallen from the ax, and she said to an aged man whom she had comforted as they ascended the scaffold, "Go first, that you may not witness my death," and then undaunted, took her turn to die—that day was to her only the last act of a tragedy, of which her marriage day was the first.

The Ten Commandments Good Foundation for Character.—The Ten Commandments, which are the foundation of all good law—Roman law, German law, English law, American law—are the best foundation upon which to build character, and those which the boy, Stephen J. Field, so often heard in the parsonage at Stockbridge, were his guidance when a half-century after, as a robed justice of the Supreme Court of the United States, he unrolled his opinions. Bibles, hymn-books, catechisms, family prayers, atmosphere sanctified, are good surroundings for boys and girls to start from; and if our laxer ideas of religion and Sabbath days and home-training produce as splendid men and women as the much derided Puritanic Sabbath and Puritanic teachings have produced, it will be a matter of congratulation and thanksgiving.

Character in Handwriting.—There are those who say they can read character by handwriting. It is said that the way one writes the letter "I" reveals his egotism or modesty, and the way one writes the letter "O" decides the height and depth of his emotions. It is declared a cramped hand means a cramped nature and an easy, flowing hand a facile and liberal spirit; but if there be anything in this science, there must be some rules not yet formulated, for some of the boldest and most aggressive men have a delicate and small penmanship, while some of the most timid sign their names with the height and width and scope of the name of John Hancock on the immortal document. Some of the cleanest in person and thought present their blotted and spattered page; and some of the roughest put before us an immaculate chirography. Not our character, but the copy-plate set before us in our schoolboy days, decides the general style of our handwriting. So, also, there is a fashion in penmanship, and for one decade the letters are exaggerated and in the next minified; now erect and now aslant, now heavy and now fine. An autograph album is always a surprise, and you will find the penmanship contradicts the character of the writers. But while the chirography of the earth is uncertain, our blessed Lord in our text presents the chirography celestial. When addressing the seventy disciples standing before him, he said: "Rejoice, because your names are written in heaven."

A Weak Point in Character Injures Entire Influence.—A well-developed Christian character is a grand thing to look at. You see some men with great intellectual and spiritual proportions. You say, "How useful that man must be!" But you find amid all his splendor of faculties there is some prejudice, whim, some evil habit, that a great many people do not notice, but that is gradually spoiling that man's character; it is going to injure his entire influence.

Grace Transforms Character.—Grace often takes hold of the hardest heart and the most unlovely character and transforms it. In this Christ shows his power. It wants but little generalship to conquer a flat country, but might of artillery and heroism to take a fort manned and ready for raking cannonade. The great Captain of our salvation had forced his way into many an armed castle. I doubt not that Christ could have found many a fisherman naturally more noble hearted than Simon Peter, but there was no one by whose conversion he could more gloriously have magnified his grace. The conversion of a score of Johns would not have illustrated the power of the Holy Ghost as much as the conversion of one Peter. It would have been easier to drive twenty lambs like John into the fold than to tame one lion like Peter. God has made some of his most efficient servants out of men naturally unimpressionable. As men take unwieldy timber and under huge machinery bend it into the hulk of great ships, thus God has often shaped and bent into his service the most unwieldy natures.

CHEERFULNESS

There is a Catholicon for Everything.—Although this book may speak of griefs and wrongs, it is with full belief there is a catholicon that can cure anything, and everything. The world is very much as we make it. Show me the color of a man's spectacles and I will tell you what kind of a world it is. Blue spectacles, a blue world. Green spectacles, a green world. Yellow spectacles, a jaundiced world. Transparent spectacles, the beautiful world that God made it. The first thing is to have the heart right, the second is to have the liver right. My friend has for many years been troubled with indigestion. Desirous of cheering him up I looked out of the window and said: "That snow is beautiful." He answered: "It will turn to slush and sleet." I said, "The human body is a fine piece of mechanism." He answered: "Warts, croup, marasmus, bunions, gout and indigestion." I grew vehement and said: "You must have noticed that this is a splendid world; all the looms of heaven must have been at work on the wing of a kingfisher. What grotesque rock of the mountain hath set the streams into roisterous laughter? What harp of heaven gives the pitch of the music of the south wind? There is enough wisdom to confound the earth and the heavens in the structure of one cricket. Even the weeds of the field are dressed like the daughters of God, and men may sneer at their commonness, but have no capacity to fathom or climb or compass the infinity of beauty in a dandelion or the blossom of a potato top. On a summer night I have seen the stars of heaven and the dews of earth married, the grass-blades holding up their fingers for the setting of the wedding signet while voices from above said: 'With this ring I thee endow, with all my light, and love, and splendor celestial.' At sunset I have seen the flaming chariots of God drive down into Lake Winnepesaukee, the panting nostrils stirring the water and the spray like dust tossed from the glittering wheels." "Bosh," cried my invalid friend, "I have never seen anything like that in all my life." So handing him over a bottle of Dyspeptic Bitters, I retired to my room to consider the value of a cheerful spirit.

The World Needs Encouragement.—This is a dark world to many people, a world of chills, a world of fog, a world of wet blankets. Nine-tenths of the men we meet need encouragement. Your work is urgent, you have no time to stop and speak to the people; but every day you meet scores, perhaps hundreds of persons upon whom you might have direct and immediate influence. "How?" you cry out. We answer by the grace of physiognomy. There is nothing so catching as a face with a lantern behind it shining clear through. We have no admiration for a face with a dry smile, meaning no more than the grin of a false face. But a smile written by the hand of God, as an index or table of contents to whole volumes of good feeling within is a benediction. Freshness and geniality of soul are so subtle and pervading that they will at some eye or mouth corner, leak out.

Congratulations for Others.—May God put congratulations for others into our right hand, and cheers on our lips for those who do brave things. Life is short at the longest; let it all be filled up with helpfulness for others, work and sympathy for each other's misfortunes, and our arms be full of white mantles to cover up the mistakes and failures of others. If an evil report about some one come to us let us put on the most favorable construction, as the Rhone enters Lake Leman foul and comes out crystalline.

Fresh Air Kills Moping.—Almost every nature, however sprightly, sometimes will drop into a minor key, or a subdued mood that in common parlance is recognized as "the blues." There may be no adverse causes at work, but somehow the bells of the soul stop ringing and you feel like sitting quiet, and you strike off forty per cent from all your worldly and spiritual prospects. The immediate cause may be a north wind or a balky liver.

In such a depressed state no one can afford to sit for an hour. First of all let him get up and go out of doors. Fresh air and the faces of cheerful men and pleasant women and frolicsome children will in fifteen minutes kill moping. The first moment your friend strikes the keyboard of your soul it will ring music. On one block in Brooklyn lives a doctor, an undertaker, and a clergyman. That is not the row for a nervous man to walk on lest he soon need all three. Throw back all the shutters of your soul and let the sunshine of genial faces shine in.

Set the Sparkle Instead of the Gloom.—It would be well if not only in looking at our own condition, but at other people, we set the sparkle instead of the gloom. With five hundred faults of our own, we ought to let somebody else have at least one. When there is such excellent hunting on our own ground, let us not with rifle and grayhound pack spend all our time in scouring our neighbor's lowlands. I am afraid the imperfections of other people will kill us yet. All the vessels on the sea seem to be in bad trim except our schooner. A person full of faults is most merciless in his criticism of the faults of others. How much better like the sun to find light wherever we look, letting people have their idiosyncrasies and every one work in his own way.

We may not all of us have the means to graduate from Harvard, Yale or Oxford, but there is a college from which all of us graduate, the college of hard knocks; Misfortune, Fatigue, Exposure and Disaster are the professors; kicks, cuffs, and blows are the curriculum, the day we leave this world is our graduation; some sit down and cry, some turn their faces to the wall and pout; others stand up and conquer. Happy the bee that even under leaden skies looks for blossoming buckwheat! wise the fowl that instead of standing in the snow with one foot drawn up under the wing ceases not all day to peck.

Cheerfulness Upon a Man's Countenance.—Let Christian cheerfulness try its chisel upon a man's countenance. Those are the faces I look for in millennial glory. They are Heaven impersonated. They are the sculpturing of God's right hand. They are hosannas in human flesh. They are hallelujahs alighted. They are Christ reincarnated. I do not care what your features are or whether you look like your father or your mother, or look like no one under the heavens—to God and man you are beautiful. Michelangelo, the sculptor, visiting Florence, some one showed him in a back yard a piece of marble that was so shapeless it seemed of no use, and Angelo was asked if he could make anything out of it, and if so was told he could own it. The artist took the marble and for nine months shut himself up to work, first trying to make of it a statue of David with his foot on Goliath, but the marble was not quite long enough at the base to make the prostrate form of the giant and so the artist fashioned the marble into another figure that is to be famous for all time because of its expressiveness. A critic came in and was asked by Angelo for his criticism and he said it was beautiful but the nose of the statue was not of right shape. Angelo picked up from the floor some sand and tossed it about the face of the statue, pretending he was using his chisel to make the improvement suggested by the critic. "What do you think of it now?" said the artist. "Wonderfully improved," said the critic. "Well," said the artist, "I have not changed it at all." My friends, the grace of God comes to the heart of a man or woman and then undertakes to change a forbidding and repulsive face into attractiveness. Perhaps the face is most unpromising for the Divine Sculptor; but having changed the heart, it begins to work on the countenance with celestial chisel, and into all the lineaments of the face puts a gladness and an expectation that changes it from glory to glory, and though earthly criticism may disapprove of this or that in the appearance of the face, Christ says of the newly-created countenance that which Pilate said of him: "Behold the man!"

CHILDREN

First Ten Years.—There are no years so important for impression as the first ten. Then and there is the impression made for virtue or vice, for truth or falsity, for bravery or cowardice, for religion or skepticism. Suddenly start out from behind a door and frighten the child, and you shatter his nervous system for a lifetime. During the first ten years you can tell him enough spook stories to make him a coward until he dies. Act before him as though Friday were an unlucky day and it were baleful to have thirteen at the table, or see the moon over the left shoulder and he will never recover from the idiotic superstitions. You may give that girl before she is ten years old a fondness for dress that will make her a mere "Dummy frame" or fashion-plate for forty years. "As is the mother so is her daughter."

Before one decade has passed you can decide whether that boy shall be a Shylock or a George Peabody. Boys and girls are generally echoes of fathers and mothers. What an incoherent thing for a mother out of temper to punish a child for getting mad, or for a father who smokes to shut his boy up in a dark closet because he has found him with an old stump of a cigar in his mouth; or for that mother to rebuke her daughter for staring at herself too much in the looking-glass when the mother has her own mirrors so arranged as to repeat her form from all sides. The great English poet's loose moral character was decided before he left the nursery, and his school-master in the school-room overheard this conversation. "Byron, your mother is a fool," and he answered, "I know it." You can hear all through the heroic life of Senator Sam Houston the words of his mother, when she in the War of 1812 put a musket in his hand and said: "There, my son, take this and never disgrace it, for remember I had rather all my sons should fill one honorable grave than that one of them should turn his back on an enemy. Go and remember, too, that while the door of my cottage is open to all brave men, it is always shut against cowards." Agrippina, the mother of Nero, a murderess: you are not surprised that her son was a murderer. Give that child an overdose of catechism and make him recite verses of the Bible as a punishment and make Sunday a bore, and he will become a stout antagonist of Christianity. Impress him with the kindness and the geniality and the loveliness of religion and he will be its advocate and exemplar for all time and eternity.

On one occasion while I was traveling in the West, right before our express train on the Louisville and Nashville Railroad, the preceding train had gone down through a broken bridge, twelve cars falling a hundred feet and then consumed. I saw that only one span of the bridge was down and all the other spans were standing. Plan a good bridge of morals for your sons and daughters, but have the first span of ten years defective and through that they will crash down, though all the rest keep standing.

The Army of Children.—The country is going to be conquered by a great army, compared with which that of Xerxes, and Alexander and Grant and Lee all put together, were in number insignificant. They will capture all the pulpits, storehouses, factories, and halls of legislation, all our shipping, all our wealth and all our honors. They will take possession of all authority from the United States presidency down to the humblest constabulary—of everything between the Atlantic and the Pacific oceans. They are on the march now, and they halt neither day nor night. They will soon be here, and all the present active population of this country must surrender and give way. I refer to the great army of children. Whether they take possession of everything for good or for evil, depends upon the style of preparation through which they pass on their way from cradle to throne.

The Preface of Young Life.—Cicero acknowledged he kept in his desk a collection of prefaces for books, which prefaces he could at any time attach to anything he wanted to publish for himself or others; and all parents and teachers have all prepared the preface of every young life under their charge, and not only the preface, but the appendix, whether the volume be a poem or a farce. Families and schools, and legislatures are busily engaged in discussing what is the best mode of educating children. Before this question almost every other dwindles into insignificance, while dependent upon a solution is the welfare of government and ages eternal.

Checks and Balances.—An error prevalent in the training of children is the laying out of a theory and following it without arranging it to varieties of disposition. In every family you will find striking differences of temperament. This child is too timid, and that too bold, and one miserly, and one too wasteful, this too inactive, and that too boisterous. Now a farmer who would plant corn and wheat and turnips in just the same way, then put them through one hopper and grind them in the same mill would not be as foolish as the parents who would attempt to discipline and educate all their children in the same way. It needs a skillful hand to adjust these checks and balances. The rigidity of government which is necessary to hold in this impetuous nature would utterly crush that flexible disposition, while the gentle reproof that would suffice for the latter would, when used on the former, be like attempting to hold a champing Bucephalus with reins of gossamer.

God gives us in the disposition of each child a hint as to how we ought to train him, and as God, in the mental structure of our children, indicates what mode of training is the best, he also indicates in the disposition, their future occupation. Do not write down that child as dull because it may not now be as brilliant as the other children or as those of your neighbor. Some of the mightiest men and women of the centuries had a stupid childhood. Thomas Aquinas was called in school "the dumb ox," but afterwards demonstrated his sanctified genius and was called "the angel of the schools" and "the eagle of Brittany."

Responsibility of Children.—Two little feet started on an eternal journey, and you were to lead them, a gem to flash in heaven's coronet, and you to polish it; eternal ages of light and darkness watching the starting out of a newly created creature. You rejoiced and you trembled at the responsibility that in your possession an immortal treasure was placed. You prayed and rejoiced and wept and wondered; you were earnest in supplication that you might lead it through life into the kingdom of God. There was a tremor in your earnestness. There was a double interest about your home. There was an additional interest why you should stay there and be faithful and when in a few months your house was filled with the music of the child's laughter, you were struck through with the fact that you had a stupendous mission. Have you kept that vow? Have you neglected any of these duties?

Give the Baby a Chance.—A pioneer in California said that for the first year or two of his residence in Sierra Nevada County, there was not a single child in all the reach of a hundred miles. But the Fourth of July came, and the miners were gathered together, and they were celebrating the Fourth with oration, and poem, and a boisterous brass band, and while the band was playing an infant's voice was heard crying, and all the miners were startled, and the swarthy men began to think of their homes on the Eastern coast and of their wives and families far away, and their hearts were thrilled with homesickness as they heard the babe cry. But the music went on, and the child cried louder, and louder, and the brass band played louder and louder, trying to drown out the infantile interruption when a swarthy miner, the tears rolling down his face, got up and shook his fist and said, "Stop that noisy band, and give the baby a chance." Oh! there was pathos in it, as well as good cheer in it. There is nothing to arouse and melt and subdue the soul like a child's voice.

Children of the Poor.—Have you ever examined the faces of the neglected children of the poor? Other children have gladness in their faces. When a group of them rush across the road it seems as though a spring gust had unloosened an orchard of apple-blossoms. But the children of the poor! There is but little ring and laughter and it stops quickly, as though some bitter memory tripped it. They have an old walk. They do not skip or run up on the lumber just for the pleasure of leaping down. They never bathed in the mountain stream. They never waded in the brook for pebbles. They never chased the butterfly across the lawn, putting their hat right down where it was just before. Childhood has been dashed out of them. Want waved its wizard wand above the manger of their birth, and withered leaves are lying where God intended a budding giant of battle.

Better a Wicked Dunce than a Wicked Philosopher.—Whether knowledge is a mighty good or an unmitigated evil depends entirely upon which course it takes. The river rolling on between sound banks makes all the valley laugh with golden wheat and rank grass and catching hold of the wheel of mill and factory, whirls it with great industries. But breaking away from restraints and dashing over banks in red wrath, it washes away harvests from their moorings and makes the valleys shrink with the catastrophe. Fire in the furnace heats the house or drives the steamer; but uncontrolled, warehouses go down in awful crash before it, and in a few hours half a city will lie in ruin, walls and towers and churches and monuments. You must accompany the education of the intellect with education of the heart, or you are arousing up within your child an energy which will be blasting and terrible. Better a wicked dunce than a wicked philosopher.

Time to be Sportful.—Childhood is the time to be sportful. Let them romp and sing and laugh and go with a rush and a hurrah. In this way they gather up a surplus energy for a future life. Hush the robins in the air till they become silent as a bat, and lecture the frisking lambs on the hillside until they walk like sheep, rather than put exhilarant childhood in the stocks. The present generations of men pass off very much as they are now. Therefore to the youth we turn. Before they sow wild oats get them to sow wheat and barley. You fill the bushel measure with good corn and there will be no room for husks.

Saving a Child.—An engineer on a locomotive going across the western prairies day after day, saw a little child come out in front of a cabin and wave to him, so he got in the habit of waving back to the little child and it was the day's joy to him to see the little child come out in front of the cabin door and wave to him while he answered back. One day the train was belated and it came on to the dusk of the evening. As the engineer stood at his post he saw by the headlight that little girl on the track, wondering why the train did not come, looking for the train, knowing nothing of its peril. A great horror seized upon the engineer. He reversed the engine. He gave it in charge of the other man on board, and then he climbed over the engine and he came down on the cowcatcher. He said, though he had reversed the engine, it seemed as though it were going at lightning speed, faster and faster, though it was really slowing up, and with almost superhuman clutch he caught that child by the hair and lifted it up, and when the train stopped, and the passengers gathered around to see what was the matter, there the old engineer lay, fainted dead away, the little child alive and all unhurt in his swarthy arms. "Oh!" you say, "that was well done." But I want you to exercise some kindness and some appreciation toward those in every community who are snatching the little ones from under the wheels of temptation and sin—snatching them from under thundering rail-trains of eternal disaster, bringing them up into respectability in this world and into glory for the world to come.

CHRIST

Christ's Credentials.—Another thing the world and the church have not observed; that is, Christ's pathetic credentials. How did they know he was not a gardener? His garments said he was a gardener. The flakes of the upturned earth scattered upon his garments said he was a gardener. How do you know he was not a gardener? Before Easter had gone by He gave to some of His disciples His three credentials. A scar in the right palm, a scar in the left palm, a scar amid the ribs—scars, scars. That is the way they knew Him. That is the way you and I will know Him. Am I saying too much when I say that will be one of the ways in which you and I will know each other—by the scars of earth; scars of accident, scars of sickness, scars of persecution, scars of hard work, scars of battle, scars of old age. When I see Christ's resurrected body having scars it makes me think that our remodeled and resurrected bodies will have scars. Why, before we get out of this world some of us will be covered all over with scars.

Trials of Christ in Seeking Lost Souls.—No one cares for your soul! Have you heard how Christ feels about it? I know it was only five or six miles from Bethlehem to Calvary—the birthplace and the deathplace of Christ—but who can tell how many miles it was from the throne to the manger? How many miles down, how many miles back again? The place of his departure was the focus of all splendor and pomp. All the thrones facing His throne. His name the chorus in every song and the inscription on every banner. His landing-place a cattle-pen, malodorous with unwashed brutes, and dogs growling in and out of the stable. Born of a weary mother who had journeyed eighty miles in severe indisposition that she might find the right place for the Lord's nativity—born, not as other princes, under the flash of a chandelier, but under a lantern swung by a rope to the roof of the barn. In that place Christ started to save you. Your name, your face, your time, your eternity, in Christ's mind. Sometimes traveling on mule's back to escape King Herod's massacre, sometimes attempting nervous sleep on the chilly hillside, sometimes earning his breakfast by the carpentry of a plow. In Quarantania the stones of the field by their shape and color, looking like the loaves of bread, tantalizing His hunger. Yet all the time keeping on after you. With drenched coat treading the surf of Gennesaret. Howled after by a bloodthirsty mob. Denounced as a drunkard. Mourning over a doomed city, while others shouted at the sight of the resplendent towers. All the time coming on and coming on to save you. Indicted as a traitor against government, perjured witnesses swearing their souls away to insure his butchery. Flogged, spit on, slapped in the face, and then hoisted on rough lumber, in the sight of earth and heaven and hell, to purchase your eternal emancipation. From the first infant step to the last step of manhood on the sharp spike of Calvary a journey for you. Oh, how He cared for your soul! By dolorous arithmetic add up the stable, the wintry tempest, the midnight dampness, the abstinence of forty days from food, the brutal Sanhedrin, the heights of Golgotha, across which all the hatreds of earth and all the furies of hell charged with their bayonets, and then dare to say again that no one cares for your soul.

Christ's Bridge of Mercy.—There are in man seven devils—devil of avarice, devil of pride, devil of hate, devil of indolence, devil of falsehood, devil of strong drink, devil of impurity. God can take them all away, seven or seventy. I remember in 1884 I rode over the new cantilever bridge that spans Niagara—a bridge nine hundred feet long, eight hundred and fifty-nine feet of chasm from bluff to bluff. I passed over it without any anxiety. Why? Because on the preceding December twenty-two locomotives and twenty-two cars laden with gravel had tested the bridge, thousands of people standing on the Canadian side, thousands standing on the American side to applaud the achievement. And however long the train of our immortal interests may be, we are to remember that God's bridge of mercy spanning the chasm of sin has been fully tested by the awful tonnage of all the pardoned sin of all the ages, church militant standing on one bank, church triumphant standing on the other bank.

Joy and Laughter of Christ.—In all our Christian work you and I want more of the element of gladness. That man had no right to say that Christ never laughed. Do you suppose that he was somber at the wedding in Cana of Galilee? Do you suppose Christ was unresponsive when the children clambered over his knee and shoulder at his own invitation? Do you suppose that the evangelist meant nothing when he said of Christ: "He rejoiced in spirit"? Do you believe that the divine Christ who pours all the water over the rocks at Vernal Falls, Yosemite, does not believe in the sparkle and gallop and tumultuous joy and rushing raptures of human life? I believe not only that the morning laughs, and that the mountains laugh, and that the seas laugh, and that the cascades laugh, but that Christ laughed.

Christ's Hand.—The great artists of the ages— Raphael and Leonardo da Vinci and Quentin Matsys and Rembrandt and Albrecht Dürer and Titian—have done their best in picturing the face of Christ, but none except Ary Scheffer seems to have put much stress upon the hand of Christ. Indeed, the mercy of that hand, the gentleness of that hand, is beyond all artistic portrayal. Some of his miracles he performed by word of mouth and without touching the subject before him, but most of them he performed through the hand. Was the dead damsel to be raised to life? "He took her by the hand." Was the blind man to have his optic nerve restored? "He took him by the hand." Was the demon to be exorcised from a suffering man? "He took him by the hand." The people saw this and besought him to put his hand on their afflicted ones. His own hands free, see how the Lord sympathized with the man who had lost the use of his hand. Christ looked at that shriveled-up right hand, dangling uselessly at the man's side and then cried out with a voice that had omnipotence in it: "Stretch forth thy hand," and the record is, "he stretched it forth whole as the other."

Christ, a Victim of Jealousy.—The passion rose up and under the darkest cloud that ever shadowed the earth and amid the loudest thunder that ever shook the mountains, and amid the wildest flash of lightning that ever blinded or stunned the nations, hung up on two pieces of rough lumber back of Jerusalem the kindest, purest, lovingest nature that heaven could delegate, and stopped not until there was no power left in hammer or bramble or javelin to hurt the dead Son of God.

Christ Prematurely Old.—Christ was prematurely old. He had been exposed to all the weathers of Palestine. He had slept out-of-doors, now in the night dew and now in the tempest. He had been soaked in the surf of Lake Galilee. Pillows for others, but he had not where to lay his head. Hungry, he could not even get a fig on which to breakfast. Oh, have you missed the pathos of that verse, "In the morning, as he returned unto the city, he hungered, and when he saw a fig tree in the way he came to it and found nothing thereon." He was a hungry Christ and nothing makes the hand tremble worse than hunger; for it pulls upon the stomach and the stomach pulls upon the brain, and the brain pulls upon the nerves, and the agitated nerves make the hand quake. In addition to all this exasperation came abuse. Oh, he was a worn-out Christ. That is the reason he died so soon upon the cross. Many victims of crucifixion lived day after day upon the cross; but Christ was in the court-room at twelve o'clock of noon and he had expired at three o'clock in the afternoon of the same day. Subtracting from the three hours between twelve and three o'clock the time taken to travel from the court-room to the place of execution and the time that must have been taken in getting ready for the tragedy, there could not have been much more than two hours left. Why did Christ live only two hours upon the cross, when others had lived forty-eight hours? He was worn-out before he got there.

Witnesses.—If this world is ever brought to God it will not be through argument, but through testimony. You might cover the whole earth with apologies for Christianity, and learned treatises in defense of religion; you would not convert a soul. Lectures on the harmony between science and religion afford exquisite mental discipline, but have never saved a soul, and never will save a soul. Put a man of the world and a man of the Church against each other, and the man of the world will, in all probability, get the triumph. There are a thousand things in our religion that seem illogical to the world, and always will seem illogical. Our weapon in this conflict is faith, not logic; faith, not metaphysics; faith, not profundity; faith, not scholastic exploration. But then in order to have faith we must have testimony; and if five hundred men, or one thousand, or five hundred thousand men, or five million men get up and tell me that they have felt the religion of Jesus Christ a joy, a comfort, a help, and inspiration, I am bound, as a fair-minded man, to accept their testimony.

I want to put before you three propositions. The first proposition is: We are witnesses that the religion of Christ is able to convert a soul. The Gospel may have had a hard time to conquer us; we may have fought it back, but we were vanquished. You say conversion is only an imaginary thing. We know better. "We are witnesses." There never was so great a change in our heart and life on any other subject as on this. People laughed at the missionaries in Madagascar because they preached ten years without one convert; but there are thirty-three thousand converts in Madagascar to-day. But why go so far to find evidences of the Gospel's power to save a soul? "We are witnesses." If I should demand that all those who have felt the converting power of religion should rise, so far from being ashamed, they would spring to their feet with more alacrity than they ever sprang to the dance, the tears mingling with their exhilaration as they cried: "We are witnesses!"

Again I remark that "we are witnesses" of the Gospel power to comfort. When a man has trouble the world comes in and says: "Now get your mind off this: go out and breathe the fresh air; plunge deeper into business." What poor advice—get your mind off it! when everything is upturned with the bereavement, and everything reminds you of what you have lost. Get your mind off it! They might as well advise you to stop thinking; and you cannot stop thinking in that direction.

Did Christ come to you and say: "Get your mind off this; go out and breathe the fresh air; plunge deeper into business?" No. There was a minute when he came to you—perhaps in the watches of the night, perhaps in your place of business, perhaps along the street—and he breathed something into your soul that gave peace, rest, infinite quiet, so that you could take out the photograph of the departed one and look into the eyes of the face of the dear one and say: "It is all right; she is better off; I would not call her back. Lord, I thank thee that thou hast comforted my poor heart." There are Christian parents here who are willing to testify to the power of this Gospel to comfort. There comes from comforted widowhood and orphanage, and childlessness, "Aye, aye, we are witnesses!"

Again I remark that religion has power to give composure in the last moment. Here are people who say: "I saw a Christian father and mother die, and they triumphed." "I saw a Christian brother die, and he triumphed." And some one else: "I saw a Christian sister die, and she triumphed." Some one else will say: "I saw a Christian daughter die, and she triumphed." Come all ye who have seen the last moments of a Christian and give testimony in this case on trial. Uncover your heads, put your hand on the old family Bible, from which they used to read the promises, and promise in the presence of high heaven that you will tell the truth, the whole truth, and nothing but the truth. With what you have seen with your own eyes, and from what you have heard with your ears, is there power in this gospel to give calmness and triumph in the last extremity? The response comes from all sides, from young and old and middle-aged: "We are witnesses!"

You see, my friends, I have not put before you an abstraction, or a chimera, or anything like guesswork. I present you affidavits of the best men and women living and dead. Two witnesses in court will establish a fact. Here are not two witnesses, but thousands of witnesses—millions of witnesses; and in heaven a great multitude of witnesses that no man can number, testifying that there is power in this religion to convert the soul, to give comfort in trouble, and to afford composure in the last hour.

CHURCH

What is a Church?—If you ask fifty men what a church is they would give you fifty answers.

One man would say "It is a convention of hypocrites." Another would say "It is an assembly of people who feel themselves a great deal better than others." Another "It is a place for gossip, where wolverine dispositions devour each other." Another "It is an art gallery, where men go to admire grand arches and exquisite fresco and musical warble and the Dantesque in gloomy imagery." Another "It is a place for the cultivation of superstition and cant." Another man would say "It is the best place on earth except my own home." "If I forget thee, O Jerusalem, let my right hand forget her cunning."

Now whatever a church is, it ought to be—a great practical, homely, omnipotent help. "Send thee help from the sanctuary." The pew ought to yield restfulness for the body. The upholstery ought to yield pleasure to the eye. The entire service ought to yield strength for the toil and struggle of everyday life. The Sabbath ought to be harnessed to all the six days of the week, drawing them in the right direction. Every man gets roughly jostled, gets abused, gets cut, gets insulted, gets slighted, gets exasperated. By the time the Sabbath comes he has an accumulation of six days' annoyances; and that is a starving church service which has not strength enough to take that accumulated annoyance and hurl it into perdition. The business man sits down in church headachy from the week's engagements. Perhaps he wishes he had tarried at home on the lounge with the newspapers and the slippers. That man wants to be cooled off, and graciously diverted. The wave of religious service ought to dash clear over the hurricane-decks, and leave him dripping with holy, and glad, and heavenly emotion. "Send thee help from the sanctuary."

Help ought to come from the music. Sabbath song ought to set all the week to music. We want not more harmony, not more artistic expression, but more volume in our church music. I am not a worshiper of noise, but I believe that if American churches would with full heartiness of soul and full emphasis of voice sing the songs of Zion, this part of sacred worship, would have tenfold more power than it has now.

Suppose each person in an audience brought all the annoyance of the last three hundred and sixty-five days. Fill the room to the ceiling with sacred song, and you would drown out all those annoyances of the last three hundred and sixty-five days and you would drown them out forever. Let the voice fall into line, and in companies and regiments by storm take the obduracy and sin of the world. If you cannot sing for yourself, sing for others. By trying to give others good cheer you will bring good cheer to your own heart.

Help ought to come from the sermon. Of a thousand people in any audience how many want sympathetic help? Do you guess one hundred? Do you guess five hundred? You have guessed wrong. I will tell you just the proportion. Out of a thousand people in any audience there are just one thousand who need sympathetic help. The young people want it just as much as the old. The old people sometimes seem to think they have a monopoly of the rheumatisms and the neuralgias and the headaches and the physical disorders of the world; but I tell you there are no worse heart-aches than are felt by some of the young people.

I have noticed amid all classes of men some of the severest battles and the toughest work come before thirty. Therefore we must have our sermons and our exhortations all sympathetic with the young, and with people further on in life. What do these doctors and lawyers and merchants and mechanics care about the abstractions of religion? What they want is help to bear the whimsicalities of patients, the browbeating of legal opponents, the unfairness of customers; they have plenty of faultfinding for every imperfection of handiwork but no praise for twenty excellences.

While all of a sermon may not be helpful alike to all, if it be a Christian sermon preached by a Christian man there will be help somewhere. All the parts may not be appropriate to our case but if we wait prayerfully, before the sermon is through we shall have the divine prescription.

When the impression is confirmed that our churches, by architecture, by music, by sociability, and by sermon shall be made the most attractive places on earth then we will want twice as many churches as we have now—twice as large—and then they will not half accommodate the people.

The old style church will not do the work. We might as well now try to take all the passengers from Washington to New York by stage coach, all the passengers from Albany to Buffalo by canal boat, as with the old style church to meet the exigencies of this day. Unless the church of this day will adapt itself to the time, it will become extinct. The people reading newspapers, and books all the week in alert picturesque and resounding style will have no patience with Sabbath humdrum. We have no objection to surpluses and all the paraphernalia of clerical life; but these things make no more impression on the great masses of the people than the ordinary business suit you wear on Pennsylvania Avenue or Wall Street. A tailor cannot make a minister. Some of the poorest ministers we know wear the best clothes; and many a backwoodsman has dismounted from his saddle bags and in his linen duster preached a sermon that shook the earth and Heaven with its Christian eloquence. No new gospel only the old gospel in a way suited to the time.

You and I tarry here only a brief space. We want

somebody to teach us how to get out of this life at the right time and in the right way. Some fall out of this life; some go stumbling out of life; some go groaning out of life; some go cursing out of life. We want to go singing, rising, rejoicing. We want to know how to get ashore from the tumult of this world into the land of everlasting peace. We do not want to stand doubting and shivering when we go away from this world; we want our anticipations aroused to the highest pitch.

Criticism of the Church.—The fragrance of spikenard, the flash of jewels, the fruitfulness of orchards, the luxuriance of gardens, the beauty of Heshbon fish-pools, the dew of the night, the splendor of the morning—all contribute to Solomon's style when he comes to speak of the glory of the Church. In contrast to his eulogium of the Church, look at the denunciatory things that are said in our day regarding it. If one stockholder becomes a cheat, does that destroy a whole company? If one soldier be a coward, does that condemn the whole army? And yet there are many in this day so unphilosophic, so illogical, so dishonest, and so unfair, as to denounce the entire Church of God because there are here and there unworthy men belonging to it.

Candlesticks Without Candles.—Cromwell stabled his cavalry horses in St. Paul's Cathedral, and many now use the church as a place in which to stable vanities and worldliness. A worldly church is a candlestick without a candle, and it had its prototype in St. Sophia, in Constantinople, built to the glory of God by Constantine, but transformed to base uses by Mohammed II. Built out of colored marble; a cupola with twenty-four windows soaring to the height of one hundred and eighty feet; the ceiling one great bewilderment of mosaic; galleries supported by eight columns of porphyry and sixty-seven columns of green jasper; nine bronze doors with alto-relievo work, fascinating to the eye of any artist; vases and vestments encrusted with all manner of precious stones. Four walls on fire with indescribable splendor. Though labor was cheap, the building cost one million, five hundred thousand dollars. Ecclesiastical structure, almost supernatural in pomp and majesty. But Mohammedanism tore down from the walls of the high building all the saintly and Christly images, and high up in the dome the figure of the cross was rubbed out that the crescent of the barbarous Turk might be substituted. A great church, but no Christ! A gorgeous candlestick but no candle! Ten thousand such churches would not give the world as much light as one homemade tallow candle by which last night some grandmother in the eighties put on her spectacles and read the Psalms of David in large type. Up with the churches by all means. Hundreds of them, thousands of them, and the more the better. But let each one be a blaze of heavenly light, making the world brighter and brighter till the last shadow has disappeared, and the last of the suffering children of God shall have reached the land where they have no need of candlestick or "of candlestick, neither light of the sun, for the Lord God giveth them light and they shall reign forever and ever!"

No Rivalries.—There should be no rivalry between churches. Each one does a work peculiar to itself. There should be no rivalry between ministers. God never repeats himself, and he never makes two ministers alike, and each has a work that no other man in the universe can accomplish.

Uncomfortable Church Pews.—In the house of God let all Christian faces beam with a look that means welcome. Why, you should be to that man a panel of the door of heaven; you should be to him a note of the doxology that seraphs sing when a new soul enters heaven. Just one word of brotherly kindness from you would lift him into a small heaven. I have in other days entered a pew in church and the woman at the other end of the pew looked at me as much as to say: "How dare you? This is my pew and I pay the rent for it!" Well, I crouched in the other corner and made myself as small as possible and felt as though I had been stealing something. So there are people who have a sharp edge to their religion and they act as though they thought most people had been elected to be damned and they were glad of it.

Christian Life a Combat.—"Masterly retreat" is a term often used in military circles, but in religion there is no such thing. It is either glorious advance or disgraceful and ignominious falling back. "Go forward" was the order given to the Israelites by the Lord through Moses.

I admit that you cannot become a Christian without a struggle; but what do you get without fighting for it? The fortresses of darkness are to be taken by storm. You may by acute strategy flank the hosts of temptation; but there are temptations, there are evils, in the way that you will have to meet face to face, and it will be shot for shot, gun for gun, grip for grip, slaughter for slaughter. The Apostle Paul, over and over again represents the Christian life as a combat. When the war vessel of Christ's Church comes into glory, bringing its crew, and its passengers, it will not come in like a North River yacht, beautifully painted and adorned, swinging into the boathouse after a pleasure excursion. Oh, no, it will be like a vessel coming with a heavy cargo from China or India, the marks of the wave and the hurricane upon it—sails rent, rigging spliced, pumps all working to keep her afloat, bulwarks knocked away.

It will come bearing upon it the marks of a great stress of weather. You can see by the very looks of that soul as it comes to glory that it was driven by the storm and dashed by the hurricane; but by so much as the voyage was rough the harbor will be blessed.

Bigóts.—I sometimes see in the church of the Lord Jesus Christ a strange thing going on; church against church, minister against minister, denomination against denomination, firing away into friend's fort, or the fort which ought to be on the same side, instead of concentrating their energy, and giving one mighty and everlasting volley against the navies of darkness riding up through the bay. I go out in the summer, and I find two beehives, and these two hives are in a quarrel. I come near enough not to be stung, but I come just near enough to hear the controversy, and one beehive says: "That field of clover is the sweetest," and another beehive says: "That field of clover is the sweetest." I come in between them and I say: "Stop this quarrel; if you like that field of clover best, go there; if you like that other field of clover best, go there, but let me tell you that that hive which gets the most honey is the best hive." So I come out between the churches of the Lord Jesus Christ. One denomination of Christians says: "That field of Christian doctrine is best," and another says: "This field of Christian doctrine is best." Well, I say: "Go where you get the most honey." That is the best church which gets the most honey, of Christian grace for the heart, and the most honey of Christian usefulness for the life.

The Triumph of the Christian Church.—In order to be qualified to meet your duty in this particular age, you want unbounded faith in the triumph of the truth and in the overthrow of wickedness. How dare the Christian Church ever get discouraged? Have we not the Lord on our side? How long did it take God to slay the hosts of Sennacherib or burn Sodom or shake down Jericho? How long will it take God when he once rises in his strength to overthrow all the forces of iniquity? Between that time and this there may be long seasons of darkness, the chariot wheels of God's Gospel may seem to drag heavily; but there is the promise, and yonder is the throne, and when Omniscience has lost its eyesight and Omnipotence falls back impotent and Jehovah is driven from his throne then the Church of Jesus Christ can afford to be discouraged, but never until then.

Despots may plan, and armies may march, and the congresses of the nations may seem to think they are adjusting all the affairs of the world, but the kings of the earth are only the dust of the chariot wheels of God's providence. And I hope before the sun of this century shall have set the last tyranny will fall and with a splendor of demonstration that shall be the astonishment of the universe, God will set forth the brightness and pomp and glory and perpetuity of his eternal government. Out of the starry flags and the emblazoned insignia of this world God will make a path for his own triumph, and, returning from universal conquest, he will sit down, the grandest, strongest, highest throne of earth his footstool.

Revision of Creeds.—I am so glad that after the Lord raised Lazarus he went on, and commanded the loosening of the cords that bound his feet so that he could walk, and the breaking off of the cerement that bound his hands so that he could stretch out his arms in salutation, and the tearing off of the bandage from around his jaw so that he could speak. What would resurrected life have been to Lazarus if he had not been freed from all those cripplements of his body: I am glad Christ commanded his complete emancipation, saying, "Loose him, and let him go."

The unfortunate thing now is that so many Christians are only half-liberated. They have been raised from the death and burial of sin into spiritual life, but they yet have the grave-clothes on them. They are like Lazarus, hobbling up the stairs of the tomb bound hand and foot.

Some are bound hand and foot by religious creeds. Let no man misinterpret me as antagonizing creeds. I have eight or ten of them; a creed about religion, a creed about art, a creed about social life, a creed about the government, and so on. A creed is something a man believes, whether it is written or unwritten.

What a time we have had with the dogmatics, the apologetics and the hermeneutics. The defect in some of the creeds is that they try to tell us all about the decrees of God. Now the only human being that was ever competent to handle that subject was Paul, and he would not have been competent had he not been inspired. I believe in the sovereignty of God, and I believe in man's free agency, but no man can harmonize them. Every sermon that I have ever heard that attempted such harmonization was to me as clear as mud. My brother of the nineteenth century, my brother of the sixteenth century, give me Paul's statement and leave out your own. Better one chapter of Paul on that subject than all of Calvin's Institutes, able and honest, and mighty as they are. Do not try to measure either the throne of God or the thunderbolts of God with your little steel pen. What do you know about the decrees? You cannot pry open the door of God's eternal counsels. You cannot explain the mysteries of God's government now; much less the mysteries of his government five hundred quintillion of years ago.

I move for a creed for all our denominations made out of Scripture quotations pure and simple. That would take the earth for God. That would be impregnable against infidelity and Apollyonic assault. That would be beyond human criticism. The denomination, whatever its name be, that can rise up to that, will be the Church of the millennium, will swallow up all other denominations, and be the one that will be the bride when the Bridegroom cometh. Let us make it simpler and plainer for the people to get into the Kingdom of God. Do not hinder people by the idea they may not have been elected. Do not tag on to the one essential faith in Christ any of the innumerable non-essentials. A man who heartily accepts Christ is a Christian, and the man who does not accept him is not a Christian, and that is all there is of it. He need not believe in election or reprobation. He need not believe in the eternal generation of the Son. He need not believe in everlasting punishment. He need not believe in infant baptism. He need not believe in plenary inspiration. Faith in Christ is the criterion, is the test, is the pivot, is the indispensable.

But there are those who would add unto the tests rather than subtract from them. There are thousands who would not accept persons into the church membership if they drink wine, or if they smoke cigars, or if they attend the theater, or if they play cards, or if they drive a fast horse. Now I do not drink wine, or smoke, or attend the theater, never played a game of cards, and do not drive a fast horse, although I would if I owned one. But do not substitute tests which the Bible does not establish. There is one passage of Scripture wide enough to let all in who ought to enter, and keep out all who ought to be kept out; "Believe in the Lord Jesus Christ and thou shalt be saved." Get a man's heart right and his life will be right.

But now that the old creeds have been put under public scrutiny, something radical must be done. Some would split them, some would carve them, some would elongate them, some would abbreviate them. At the present moment and in the present shape they are a hindrance. Lazarus is alive, but hampered with the old grave-clothes. If you want one glorious Church, free and unencumbered, take off the cerements of old ecclesiastical vocabulary. Loose her, and let her go.

There are Christians who are under sepulchral shadows, and hindered and hobbled by doubts and fears and sins long repented of. What they need is to understand the liberty of the sons of God. They spend more time under the shadow of Sinai than at the base of Calvary.

What many Christians most need is to get your grave-clothes off. O rejoice that you have been brought from the death of sin to the life of the Gospel; but you need to get your hand loose and your feet loose and your soul loose.

COMPANIONSHIP

Young Men Urged to Seek Elevating Company.— Young man, seek only elevating and improving companionship. Do not let the last scion of a noble family, a fellow with a big name but bad habits, if he drinks and swears and is dissolute, take your arm to walk down the street, or spend an evening with you, either at your room or his room. Remember that sin is the most expensive thing in

God's universe. I have read that Sir Basil, the Knight tired out with the chase, had a falcon on his wrist, as they did in days of falconry, when with hawks or falcons they went forth to bring down partridges or grouse or pigeons, and being very thirsty, came to a stream struggling from a rock, and releasing the falcon from his wrist he took the bugle which he carried, and stopping the mouth-piece of his bugle with a tuft of moss, he put this extemporized cup under the water which came down, drop by drop, from the rock until the cup was full, and then lifted it to drink, when the falcon he had released, with sudden swoop dashed the cup from his hand. By the same process he filled the cup again, and was about to drink when the falcon by another swoop dashed the cup. Enraged at this insolence and violence of the bird, he cried, "I will wring thy neck if thou doest that again." But having filled the cup a third time and trying to drink, a third time the falcon dashed it down. Then Sir Basil with his fist struck the bird, which fluttered and looked lovingly and reproachfully at him and dropped dead. Then Sir Basil looking up to the top of the rock whence dripped the water, saw a great green serpent, coiled fold above fold, the venom from his mouth dropping into that from which Sir Basil had filled his cup. Then exclaimed the knight, "What a kind thing it was for the falcon to dash down that poisoned cup, and what a sad thing that I killed him, and what a narrow escape I had." So now there are certainly no more waters that refresh than waters that poison. This moment there are thousands of young men, unwittingly, and not know-ing what they do, taking into their bugle-cup of earthly joy that which is deadly because it drips from the jaws of that old serpent, the devil, and the dove of God's Spirit in kindly warning dashes down the cup; but again it is filled and again dashed down, and again filled and again dashed down. Why not turn away and slake your thirst at the clear, bright, perennial fountain that breaks from the Rock of Ages, a fountain so wide and so deep that all the inhabitants of earth, and all the armies of heaven, may stoop down and fill their chalices?

Youthful Companionship Good for Old.—Set back the clock of human life. People make themselves old by always talking about being old, and wishing for the good old days, which were never as good as these days. From all I can hear the grandchildren are not half as bad as the grandparents were. Matters have been hushed up. But if you ever have been in a room adjoining a room where some very old people a little deaf were talking over old times you will find that this age does not monopolize all the young rascals. Revive your remembrance of what you were between five and ten years of age, and with patience capable of everything join with the young. Put back the shadow of the dial not ten degrees, but fifty and sixty and seventy degrees. In our desire to inspire the young we have had in our essays much to say about what had been accomplished by the young; of Romulus who founded Rome when he was twenty years of age; of Cortez who had conquered Mexico at thirty years; of Pitt who was prime minister of England at twenty-four years; of Raphael who died at thirty-seven years; of Calvin who wrote his Institutes at twenty-six; of Melanchthon who took a learned professor's chair at twenty-one years; of Luther who had conquered Germany for the Reformation by the time he was thirty-five years. And it is all very well for us to show how early in life one can do very great things for God and the welfare of the world, but some of the mightiest work for God has been done by septuagenarians and octogenarians and nonagenarians.

Indeed there is work which none but such can do. They preserve the equipoise of Senates, of religious denominations, of reformatory movements. Young men for action, old men for counsel.

COMPENSATION

Looking for One Thing We Find Another.—While studying the life of Columbus I am reminded of the fact that while we are diligently looking for one thing we find another. Columbus started to find India, but found America. Go on and do your duty diligently and prayerfully, and if you do not find what you looked for, you will find something better. Saul was hunting for the strayed animals of his father's barnyard, but met Samuel, the prophet who gave him a crown of dominion. Nearly all the great inventions and discoveries were made by men who at the time were looking for something else. Professor Morse, gone to Europe to perfect himself in chemistry, on returning happens to take the packership *Sully* from Havre and while in conversation with a passenger learns of some experiments in France which suggest to him the magnetic telegraphy. He went to Europe to learn the wisdom of others and discovered the telegraph. Hargreaves by the upsetting of a machine and the motion of its wheels while upset discovered the spinning-jenny. Oh, my friend, go on faithfully and promptly with your work and if you do not get the success you seek, and your plans upset, you will get something just as good, perhaps better. Sail ahead on the voyage of life, keep a correct log book, brave the tempest, make the best use of the east wind, keep a sharp lookout and I warrant you in the name of the God of Columbus that if you do not find just what you want of an earthly nature you will find heaven and that will be better. What was worn-out

India, crouching under a tropical sun, compared with salubrious and radiant and almost illimitable America; and what is all that this little world of which we live can afford you compared with that supernal realm whose foliage and whose fruits and whose riches and whose Christ make up an affluence that the most rapturous vocabulary fails to utter?

Another look at the career of that Admiral of the *Santa Maria* persuades me that it is not to be expected that this world will do its hard workers full justice. If any man ought to have been treated well from first to last it was Columbus. He had his faults. Let others depict them. But a greater soul the centuries have not produced. This continent ought to have been called Columbia, after the hero who discovered it, or Isabelliana, after the queen who furnished the means for the expedition. No. The world did not do him justice while he was alive and why should it be expected to do him justice after he was dead. Columbus in a dungeon! What a thought.

The world knows little or nothing of the bravest words and the bravest deeds. Be not surprised if you suffer injustice. You are in the best of company; the men and women who wrought mightily for God and the world's improvement, got for it chiefly misrepresentation and abuse while they lived, although afterward they had a long row of carriages at the obsequies. Do your full duty, expecting no appreciation in this world, but full reward in the world to come.

The Day of Reward Comes.—Christ, hounded of persecutors, denied a pillow, worse maltreated than the thieves on either side of the cross, human hate smacking its lips in satisfaction after it had been draining his last drop of blood, the sheeted dead bursting from the sepulchers at his crucifixion. Tell me, O Gethsemane and Golgotha, were there ever darker times than those? Like the booming of the midnight sea against the gates of eternity to be echoed back by all the thrones of heaven and all the dungeons of hell. But the day of reward comes for Christ; all the pomp and dominion of this world are to be hung on his throne, crowned heads are to bow before him on whose head are many crowns, and all celestial worship is to come up at his feet, like the humming of the forest, like the rushing of the waters, like the thundering of the seas, while all heaven rising on their thrones, beat time with their scepters. "Hallelujah, for the Lord God Omnipotent reigneth! Hallelujah, for the kingdoms of this world have become the kingdoms of our Lord Jesus Christ!"

CONCUSSION

Concussion is Messianic.—Christ's mausoleum was opened by concussion. It was a great earthquake that put its twisted key into the involved and labyrinthine lock of that tomb. Concussion! That is the power that opens all the tombs that are opened at all—tomb of the soul and tomb of the nations. Concussion between iceberg and iceberg, between bowlder and bowlder, and a thousand other concussions put this world into shape for man's residence. Concussion between David and his enemies, and out came the Psalms, which otherwise would never have been written. Concussion between God's will and man's will and, ours overthrown, we become new creatures in Christ Jesus! Concussion of misfortune and trial for many of the good, and out comes their consecration.

Do not be frightened therefore when you see the great upheavals, the great agitations, the great earthquakes, whether among the rocks, or among the nations, or in individual experience. Out of them God will bring results and most magnificent consequences. Concussion! If ever a general European war, which the world has been expecting for so many years, should come, a concussion so wide, and so tremendous would not leave a throne in Europe standing as it is now. The nations of the world are tired of having their kings born to them, and they would after a while elect their kings and there would be an Italian republic, and a German republic, and a Russian republic, and an Austrian republic, and out of the cracks and chasms of that concussion would come resurrection for all Europe. Stagnation is deathful; concussion is Messianic.

CONSOLATION

Birds Released at Tomb in the Orient.—In the East they take a cage of birds and bring it to the tomb of the dead, and then they open the door of the cage, and the birds, flying out, sing. And I would to-day bring a cage of Christian consolations to. the grave of your loved ones, and I would open the door and let them fill all the air with the music of their voices.

The Sorrowing Tree.—There is near Bombay a tree that they call the "sorrowing tree," the peculiarity of which is it never puts forth any bloom at daytime, but in the night puts out all its bloom and all its redolence. And I have to tell you that though Christian character puts forth its sweetest blossoms in the darkness of sickness, the darkness of financial distress, the darkness of bereavement, the darkness of death, "Weeping may endure for a night, but joy cometh in the morning."

Our Divine Rock.—A tree when it is in full leafage drops a great deal of refreshment; but in a little while the sun strikes through and you keep shifting position, until after a while the sun is set at such a point that you have no shade at all. But go in the heart of some great rock, such as you see in Yosemite or the Alps, and there is everlasting shadow. There has been thick shade there for six thousand years and will be for the next six thousand years. So our divine rock, once covering us always covers us. The same yesterday, to-day and forever! Always good, always kind, always sympathetic! The rock in the mountains with fingers of everlasting stone, holds its own shadow. So God's sympathy needs no holding up for us. Though we are too weak from sickness or trouble to do anything but lie down, over us he stretches the shadow of His benediction. Instead of standing right out in the blistering noon-day sun of earthly trial and trouble, come under the Rock. You may drive into it the longest caravan of disasters. There is room for the suffering, heated, sunstruck, dying of all generations in the shadow of the great Rock.

Troubles are Revelations.—There is comfort in the thought that all our troubles are a revelation. Have you ever thought of it in that connection? The man who has never been through chastisement is ignorant about a thousand things in his soul he ought to know. For instance, here is a man who prides himself on his cheerfulness of character. He has no patience with anybody who is depressed in spirits. Oh, it is easy for him to be cheerful with his fine house, his filled wardrobe and well-strung instruments of music and tapestried parlor and plenty of money in the bank waiting for some permanent investment. But suppose his fortune goes to pieces and his house goes down under the sheriff's hammer and the banks will not have anything to do with his paper. Suppose those people who were once entertained at his table get so short-sighted that they cannot recognize him upon the street.

How then? Is it so easy to be cheerful? It is easy to be cheerful in the home after the day's work is done and the gas is turned on and the house is full of romping little ones. But suppose the piano is shut because the fingers that played it will no more touch the keys, and the childish voice that asked so many questions will ask no more. Then is it so easy? My friends, those of us who have been through trouble know what a sinful and rebellious heart we have, and how much God has to put up with and how much we need pardon. It is only in the light of a flaming furnace that we can learn our own weakness and our own lack of moral resource.

Recognition in Heaven.—We read in the first book of the Bible, Abraham died and was gathered to his people. Isaac died and was gathered to his people. Jacob died and was gathered to his people. What people? Why, their friends, their comrades, their old companions. Of course it means that. It cannot mean anything else. So in the very beginning of the Bible four times that is taken for granted. The whole New Testament is an arbor over which the doctrine creeps like a luxuriant vine full of the purple clusters of consolation. James, John and Peter followed Christ into the mountains. A light falls from heaven on that mountain and lifts it into the glories of the celestial. Christ's garments glow and his face shines like the sun. The door of heaven swings open. Two spirits come down and alight on that mountain. The disciples look at them and recognize them as Moses and Elias. Now, if those disciples standing on the earth could recognize these two spirits who had been for hundreds of years in heaven, do you tell me that we, with our heavenly eyesight, will not be able to recognize those who have gone out from among us only five, ten, twenty, thirty years before?

Light From the Promises.—The eternal constellations from their circuit about God's throne, poured down an infinite luster. Under their shining, the billows of trouble took on crests and plumes of gold and jasper and amethyst and flame. All the trees of life rustled in the midsummer air of God's love. The night-blooming assurances of Christ's sympathy filled all the atmosphere with heaven. The soul at every step seemed to start up from its feet bright-winged joys, warbling heavenward. "It is good that I have been afflicted," cries David. "The Lord gave, and the Lord hath taken away," exclaims Job. "Sorrowful, yet always rejoicing," says St. Paul. "And God shall wipe away all tears from their eyes," exclaims John in apocalyptic vision. At eventime it was light. Light from the Cross! Light from the promises! Light from the throne! Streaming, joyous, outgushing, everlasting light.

Comfort Others.—People who have not had trials themselves cannot give comfort to others. They may talk very beautifully and they may give you a great deal of poetic sentiment; but while poetry is perfume that smells sweet it makes a very poor salve. If you have a grave in a pathway, and somebody comes and covers it all over with flowers, it is a grave yet. Those who have not had grief themselves know not the mystery of a broken heart. They know not the meaning of childlessness, and the having no one to put to bed at night, or the standing in a room where every book and picture and door are full of memories—the door-mat where she sat, the cup out of which she drank—the place where she stood at the door and clapped her hands—the odd figures that she scribbled—the blocks she built into a house. Ah! no, you must have trouble yourself before you can comfort trouble in others. But come all ye who have been bereft and ye who have been comforted in your sorrows and stand around these afflicted souls and say to them: "I had that very sorrow myself. God comforted me and he will comfort you," and that will go right to the spot. In other words, to comfort others, we must have faith in God, practical experience and common sense.

Refiner's Fire.—I once went through an ax factory and I saw them take the bars of iron and thrust them into the terrible furnace. Then besweated workmen with long tongs stirred the blaze. Then they brought out a bar of iron and put it in a crushing machine and then they put it between jaws that bit it in twain. Then they put it on an anvil and there were great hammers swung by machinery each one-half a ton in weight, that went thump! thump! thump! Now God puts a soul into the furnace of trial and then it is brought out and run through the crushing machine and then it comes down on the anvil and upon it, blow after blow, until the soul cries out: "O Lord, what does all this mean?" God says: "I want to make something very useful out of you. You shall be something very useful to hew with and something to build with. It is a practical process through which I am putting you." Yes, my Christian friends, we want more tools in the church of God; not more wedges to split with. We have enough of these. What we really want is keen, sharp, well-tempered axes and if there be any other way of making them than in the hot furnace on the hard anvil and under the heavy hammer, I do not know what it is.

CROAKERS

The Good Old Days.—People in the critical mood groan after what they call the good old days. They say: "Just think of the pride of people in our time. Just look at the ladies' hats!" Why, there is nothing in the ladies' hats of to-day to equal the coal-scuttle hats of a hundred years ago. They say, "Just look at the way people dress their hair!" But the extremist style of to-day will never equal the top-knots which our great-grandmothers wore put up with high combs that we would have thought would have made our great-grandfathers die of laughter. The hair was lifted into a pyramid a foot high. On the top of that tower lay a white rosebud. Shoes of bespangled white kid and heels two or three inches high. Grandfather went out to meet her on the floor with coat of sky-blue silk and vest of white satin, embroidered with gold lace, lace ruffles around his wrist and his hair falling in a queue. O ye modern hair-dressers, stand aghast at the locks of our ancestry! They say our ministers are all askew, but just think of our clergymen entering a pulpit with their hair fixed up in the shape of some of the ancient bishops. The great George Washington had his horses' hoofs blackened when about to appear on a parade, and wrote to Europe, ordering sent for the use of himself and family, "one silver-laced hat, one pair of silver shoe buckles, a coat made of fashionable silk, one pair of gold sleeve buttons, six pairs of kid gloves, one dozen most fashionable cambric pocket handkerchiefs," besides ruffles and tucker. Talk about dissipations, ye who have ever seen the old-fashioned sideboard! Did I not have an old relative who always, when visitors came, used to go upstairs and take a drink, through economical habits not offering anything to his visitors. On the old-time training days the most sober men were apt to take a day to themselves. Many of the fancy drinks of to-day were unknown to them, but their hard cider, mint julep, metheglin, hot toddy and lemonade in which the lemon was not at all prominent, sometimes made lively work for the broad-brimmed hats and silver knee buckles. Talk of dissipating parties of to-day and keeping of late hours! Why, did they not have their husking bees and sausage-stuffings and tea parties and dances that for heartiness and uproar utterly eclipsed all the waltzes, lances, redowas and breakdowns of the nineteenth century? And they never went home till morning! And as to the old-time courtships, oh, my! Washington Irving describes them. Talk about the dishonesties of to-day! Why, sixty years ago the Governor of New York State had to disband the Legislature because of its utter corruption. Think of Aaron Burr, Vice-president of the United States, and coming within one vote of being President! Think of the ministry having in it such as Dean Swift and Sterne! The world was then such a bad place that I do not see how our fathers and mothers could have been induced to stay in it, although on our account I am glad they consented.

DETERMINATION

Jonah Versus Leviathan.—Unbelievers have often told us that the story of the prophet swallowed by a great fish was an absurdity. They say that so long in the stomach of the monster, the minister would have been digested. We have no difficulty in this matter. Jonah was a most unwilling guest of the whale. He wanted to get out. However much he may have liked fish, he did not want it three times a day and all the time. So he kept up a fidget and a struggle, and a turning over and he gave the whale no time to masticate him. The man knew that if he was ever to get out he must be in perpetual motion. We know men who are so lethargic they would have given the matter up and lain down so

quietly that in a few hours they would have gone
into flukes, and fish bones, blow-holes and blubber.

Now we see men all around us who have been
swallowed by monstrous misfortune. They float out
to sea, and are never again heard of. Others the
moment they go down the throat of some great
trouble, begin immediately to plan egress. They
make rapid estimate of the length of the vertebræ,
and come to the conclusion how far they are in.
They dig up enough spermaceti out of the darkness
to make a light and keep turning this way and that,
till the first thing you know they are out.

Determination to get well has much to do with
recovered invalidism. Firm will to defeat bankruptcy decides financial deliverance. Never surrender to misfortune or discouragement. You can
be spry enough, make it as uncomfortable for the
whale as the whale can make it uncomfortable for
you. There will be some place where you can brace
your foot against his ribs and some long upper tooth
around which you can take hold, and he will be as
glad to get rid of you as a tenant as you are to get
rid of him as a landlord. There is a way if you are
determined to find it. All my sympathies are with
the plaintiff in the suit of Jonah versus Leviathan.

DISSIPATION

Minstrels of Dissipation.—Sybaris was a great
city, and it once sent out three hundred horsemen
in battle. They had a minstrel who had taught the
horses of the army a great trick, and when the old
minstrel played a certain tune, the horses would
rear and with their front feet seem to beat time to
the music. Well, the old minstrel was offended with
his country, and he went over to the enemy, and he
said to the enemy: "You give me the mastership of
the army and I will destroy the troops when those

horsemen come from Sybaris. So they gave the old minstrel the management, and he taught all the other minstrels a certain tune. Then when the cavalry troop came up the old minstrel and all the other minstrels played a certain tune and at the most critical moment in the battle when the horsemen wanted to rush to the conflict, the horses reared and beat time to the music with their forefeet, and in disgrace and rout the enemy fled.'' Ah, my friends, I have seen it again and again—the minstrels of pleasure, the minstrels of dissipation, the minstrels of godless association have defeated people in the hardest fight of life.

Evil Habits.—There is a captivity more galling than the one in which Daniel was transported; it is the captivity of evil habits. Men do not go into that wittingly. Slyly and imperceptibly are the chains forged upon them. Cyrus afterward consented that some of his captives should return, and fifty thousand of them accepted the opportunity; but tell me what evil habit ever consented to let a man go. Ten plagues made Pharaoh consent to the departure of God's people; but tell me what Pharaoh of evil habit ever cheerfully consented to let any of its victims go. Men talk of evil habits as though they were light and trivial; but they are scorpion whips that tear the flesh; they are spikes more bloody than the path of a Brahmin; they make the poisonous robe of Nessus; they are the sepulchers in which millions are buried alive.

The First Step Comparatively Easy.—The first five years of a dissipated life is comparatively easy, for it is all downhill; but when the man wakes up and finds his tongue wound with blasphemy and his eyes swimming in rheum and the antennæ of vice feeling along his nerves and he resolves to return he finds it hard traveling, for it is up hill and the fortresses along the road open on him their batteries. We go into sin hop, skip and jump; we come out of it creeping on all fours. It is smooth all the way there, and rough all the way back. For Robert Burns it is rich wine and clapping hands and carnival all the way going to Edinburgh; but going back, it is worn out body, and lost estate, and stinging conscience, and broken heart, and a drunkard's grave.

Life to Some Like a Masquerade Ball.—To many life is a masquerade ball. As at such entertainment men and women appear in garb of kings and queens or mountain bandits or clowns, and then at the close of the dance put off their disguise; so many all through life are in mask. The masquerade ball goes on, and gemmed hand clasps gemmed hand, and dancing feet respond to dancing feet, and gleaming brow bends to gleaming brow and the masquerade ball goes bravely on. But after a while languor comes and blurs the sight. Lights lower. Floor hollow with sepulchral echo. Music saddens into wail. Lights lower. Now the masquerade is hardly seen. The fragrance is exchanged for the sickening odor of garlands that have lain a long while in the damp of sepulchers. Lights lower. Mists fill the room. The scarf drops from the shoulder of beauty, a shroud. Lights lower. Torn leaves and withered garlands. Choking dampness. Chilliness. Feet still. Hands folded. Eyes shut. Voices hushed. Lights out.

A Giant May Be Slain by a Woman.—Behold, how a giant may be slain of a woman. Delilah started the train of circumstances that pulled down the temple of Dagon about Samson's ears. Tens of thousands of giants have gone down to death and hell through the same impure fascinations. It seems to me that it is high time that pulpit and platform and printing-press speak out against the impurities of modern society. Fastidiousness and Prudery say: "Better not speak—you will rouse up adverse criticism; you will make worse what you want to make better; better deal in glittering generalities; the subject is too delicate for polite ears." But there comes a voice from heaven overpowering the mincing sentimentalities of the day, saying: "Cry aloud, spare not, lift up thy voice like a trumpet, and show my people their transgressions and the house of Jacob their sins." The trouble is that when people write or speak upon this theme they are apt to cover it up with the graces of belles-lettres, so that the crime is made attractive instead of repulsive. Lord Byron in "Don Juan" adorns this crime until it smiles like a May queen. Michelet, the great French writer, covers it up with bewitching rhetoric until it glows like the rising sun, when it ought to be loathsome as a smallpox hospital.

DIVINE SATIRE

Christ's Scalpel of Truth.—A proverb is compact wisdom, knowledge in chunks, a library in a sentence, the electricity of many clouds discharged into one bolt, a river put through a mill-race. When Christ quotes the proverb "Ye blind guides, which strain at a gnat, and swallow a camel" he means to set forth the ludicrous behavior of those who make a great bluster about small sins and have no appreciation of the great ones. A small insect and a large quadruped are brought in comparison—a gnat and a camel. The insect spoken of is in its very smallest shape, and it inhabits the water for the proverb is a misprint and ought to read "Strain out a gnat."

While Christ's audience were yet smiling at the appositeness and wit of his illustration—for smile they did unless they were too stupid to understand the hyperbole—Christ practically said to them—"That is you." Punctilious about small things; reckless about affairs of great magnitude. No subject ever winced under a surgeon's knife, more bitterly than did the Pharisees under Christ's scalpel of truth As an anatomist will take a human body to pieces, and put the pieces under a microscope for examination, so Christ finds his way to the heart of the dead Pharisee and cuts it out and puts it under the glass of inspection for all generations to examine. Those Pharisees thought Christ would flatter them and compliment them and how they must have writhed under the red-hot words as he said "Ye fools, ye whited sepulchres, ye blind guides which strain out a gnat and swallow a camel." There are in our day a great many gnats strained out and a great many camels swallowed and it is my object to sketch a few persons who are extensively engaged in that business.

There are ministers of the gospel who are very scrupulous about the conventionalities of religion, but put no particular stress upon matters of vast importance. Church service ought to be grave and solemn. There is no room for frivolity in religious convocation. But there are illustrations, and there are hyperboles like that of Christ's that will irradiate with smiles any intelligent audience. There are men like those blind guides who advocate only those things in religious service which draw down the corners of the mouth, and denounce all those things which have a tendency to drag the corners of the mouth up, and these men will go to installations and to presbyteries and to conferences and to associations, their pockets full of fine sieves to strain out the gnats, while in their own churches at home every Sunday there are fifty people sound asleep. They make their churches a great dormitory, and their somniferous sermons are a cradle and drawled-out hymns a lullaby. Now I say it is worse to sleep in church than to smile in church, for the latter implies at least attention, while the former implies the indifference of the hearer, and the stupidity of the speaker.

In old age, or from physical infirmity, or from long watching with the sick, drowsiness will sometimes overpower one; but when a minister of the Gospel looks off upon an audience, and finds healthy and intelligent people struggling with drowsiness, it is time for him to give out the doxology, or pronounce the benediction. The great fault of church service to-day is not too much vivacity but too much somnolence. The one an irritating gnat that may be easily strained out; the other is a sprawling and sleepy-eyed camel of the dry desert.

I take down from my library the biographies of ministers and writers of past ages, inspired and uninspired, who have done the most to bring souls to Jesus Christ, and I find that without a single exception they consecrated their wit and their humor to Christ. Elijah used it when he advised the Baal-ites, as they could not make their god respond, to call louder, as their god might be sound asleep or gone a-hunting. Job used it when he said to his self conceited comforters, "Wisdom will die with you." Christ used it, when he described the cunning of Herod, saying "Go tell the fox" and when he ironically complimented the corrupt Pharisees, saying "The whole need not a physician." Matthew Henry's commentaries from the first page to the last coruscated with humor as summer clouds with heat lightning.

John Bunyan's writings are as full of humor as they are of saving truth, and there is not an aged man who has read "Pilgrim's Progress" who does not remember that while reading it he smiled as often as he wept. So it has been in all ages and I say to the young theological students, sharpen your wits as scimiters, and then take them into this holy war. It is a very short bridge between a smile and a tear, a suspension bridge from eye to lip, and it is soon crossed over and a smile is sometimes just as sacred as a tear. There is as much religion and I think a little more in a spring morning than in a starless night. Religious work without any humor or wit in it is a banquet with a side of beef and that raw, and no condiments, and no dessert succeeding. People will not sit down to such a banquet. By all means strain out through the sieve of holy discrimination all bathos and all lightness and vulgarity; but on the other hand beware of that monster that overshadows the Christian Church today, conventionality coming up from the Great Sahara of Ecclesiasticism, having on its back the hump of sanctimonious gloom, and vehemently refuse to swallow that camel.

Oh, how particular a great many people are about the infinitesimals while they are quite reckless about the magnitudes. What did Christ say? Did he not excoriate the people in his time who were so careful to wash their hands before a meal, but did not wash their hearts?

This subject does not give the picture of one or two persons, but it is a gallery in which thousands of people may see their likeness. For instance those people who would not rob their neighbor of a farthing—appropriate the money and the treasure of the public. A man who has a house to sell, and he tells his customer it is worth twenty thousand dollars. Next day the assessor comes around and the owner says it is worth fifteen thousand dollars.

Careful to pay their passage from Liverpool to New York, yet smuggling in their trunks silk dresses from Paris and watches from Geneva, Switzerland, telling the custom-house officer on the wharf, "There is nothing in that trunk but wearing apparel," and putting a five-dollar piece in his hand to punctuate the statement. Better swallow a thousand gnats than one camel!

Such persons are also described who are very much alarmed about the small faults of others, and have no alarm about their own great transgressions. There are in every community and in every church watch-dogs who feel called upon to keep their eyes on others and growl. They are full of suspicions. They are self-appointed detectives, always looking for something mean instead of something grand. Their neighbor's imperfections are like gnats and they strain them out; their own imperfections are like camels and they swallow them. But lest too many might think they escape the scrutiny of the proverb I have to tell you that we all come under the divine satire when we make the question of time more important than the question of eternity. Time, how small it is! Eternity, how vast it is! The former more insignificant in comparison with the latter than a gnat is insignificant when compared with a camel.

Let us all surrender to the charge. What an ado about things here. What poor preparation for a great eternity. As though a nettle were taller than a Lebanon cedar, as though a gnat were greater than a camel, as though a minute were longer than a century, as though time were higher, deeper, broader, than eternity.

That which Christ flashed with lightning of wit is followed by the crashing thunders of awful catastrophe to those who make the questions of time greater than the questions of the future, the oncoming, the overshadowing future. Eternity!

Discouragement Treated.—A great multitude of people are under seeming disadvantage, and I will to-day, in the plainest Anglo-Saxon that I can command, treat their cases; not as a nurse counts out the eight or ten drops of a prescription, and stirs them in a half-glass of water, but as when a man has by mistake taken a large amount of strychnine or Paris green or Belladonna, and the patient is walked rapidly around the room, and shaken up, until he gets wide awake. Many of you have taken a large draught of the poison of discouragement, and I come out by the order of the Divine Physician to rouse you out of that lethargy.

The Shut-in.—There are many people in the world thoroughly shut-in—some by sickness, some by old age, some by special duties that will not allow them to go forth, some surrounded by deluges of misfortune and trouble.

A hand was stretched down from heaven to close the door. It was a divine hand as well as a kind hand. "The Lord shut him in." You thought it was an accident, ascribable to the carelessness or misdoings of others, or a mere "happen-so." No! No! God had gracious designs for your betterment, for the cultivation of your patience, for the strengthening of your faith, for the advantage you might gain by seclusion, for your eternal salvation. He put you in a school room where you could learn in six months or a year more than you could have learned anywhere else in a lifetime. He turned the lattice or pulled down the blinds of the sick-room, or put your swollen foot on an ottoman, or held you amid the pillows of a couch which you could not leave, for some reason that you may not now understand, but which He has promised He will explain to you satisfactorily. If not in this world, then in the world to come, for He said: "What I do thou knowest not now, but thou shalt know hereafter."

Though the Path be Rough.—If your pathway had been smooth you would have depended upon your own sure footedness; but God roughened that path so you have to take hold of His hand. If the weather had been mild, you would have loitered along the water courses, but at the first howl of the storm you quickened your pace heavenward and wrapped around you the warm robe of a savior's righteousness. "What have I done?" says the wheat to the farmer. "What have I done that you beat me so hard with your flail?" The farmer makes no answer, but the rake takes off the straw, and the mill blows the chaff to the wind and the golden grain falls down at the foot of the windmill. After a while the straw, looking down from the mow upon the golden grain banked up on either side of the floor, understands why the farmer beats the wheat-sheaf with the flail.

Sour Experience.—In some lives the saccharine seems to predominate. Life is sunshine on a bank of flowers. A thousand hands to clap approval. In December or in January, looking across their table, they see all their family present. Health rubicund. Skies flamboyant. Days resilient. But in a great many cases there are not so many sugars as acids. The annoyances and the vexations and the disappointments of life overpower the successes.

It is absurd to suppose that a man who has always

been well can sympathize with those who are sick, or that one who has always been honored can appreciate the sorrow of those who are despised, or that one who has been born to a great fortune can understand the distress and the straits of those who are despised. The fact that Christ himself took the vinegar, makes him able to sympathize to-day and forever with all those whose cup is filled with sharp acids of this life.

He knew the sourness of betrayal. The treachery of Judas hurt Christ's feelings more than all the friendship of his disciples did him good. "They sold him for less than our twenty dollars! They all forsook him and fled. They cut him to the quick. He drank that cup to the dregs. He took the vinegar.

He knew also the sourness of pain. There are some who have not seen a well day for many years. You have struggled under a heavy mortgage of physical disabilities; and instead of the placidity that once characterized you, it is now only with great effort that you keep away from irritability and sharp retort. It is comparatively easy to fight in a regiment of a thousand men charging up the parapets to the sound of martial music, but it is not so easy to endure when no one but the nurse and the doctor are the witnesses of the Christian Fortitude. But you never had any pains worse than Christ. The sharpness that stung through his brain, through his hands, through his feet, through his heart, were as great as yours surely. He was as sick and as weary. Not a nerve or muscle or ligament escaped. All the pangs of all the nations, of all the ages compressed into one sour cup. He took the vinegar.

There is also the sourness of poverty. Your income does not meet your outgoings and that always gives an honest man anxiety. You may say nothing, but life to you is a hard push! Well, you are in glorious company. Christ owned not the house in which he stopped or the colt on which he rode, or the boat in which he sailed. He lived in a borrowed house; he was buried in a borrowed grave. Exposed to all kinds of weather, yet he had only one suit of clothes. He breakfasted in the morning, and no one could possibly tell where he could get anything to eat before night. He would have been pronounced a financial failure. He had to perform a miracle to get money to pay his tax-bill. Not a dollar did he own. Privation of domesticity—privation of nutritious food; privation of a comfortable couch on which to sleep; privation of all worldly resources. The Kings of the earth had chalices out of which to drink; but Christ had nothing but a plain cup set before him, and it was very sharp, and it was very sour.

To those to whom life has been an acerbity—a dose they could not swallow, a draught that set their teeth on edge and a rasping—I preach the omnipotent sympathy of Jesus Christ.

Brooding Wings.—In a great many places in the Psalms, David makes ornithological allusions. In Deuteronomy, God is represented as an Eagle stirring up her nest. Christ compares himself to a hen gathering the chickens under her wings; while Boaz accosts Ruth with the blessing: "A full reward be given thee of the Lord God of Israel, under whose wings thou art come to trust."

The wings of God are broad wings. They cover up all our wants, all our sorrows, all our suffering. He puts one wing over our cradle, and puts the other wing over our grave. Yes, it is not a desert in which we are placed; it is a nest. Sometimes it is a very hard nest like that of the eagle, spread on the rock, with ragged moss and rough sticks, but still it is a nest and although it may be very hard under us, over us are the wings of the Almighty.

There sometimes comes a period in one's life when he feels forsaken. Have there never been times in your life when you envied those who were buried? When you longed for the grave-digger to do his work for you? Oh, the faithlessness of the human heart! God's wings are broad, whether we know it or not.

Sometimes the mother bird goes away from the nest, and it seems strange that she should leave the callow young. She plunges her beak into the bark of the tree, and then drops into the grain field and into the chaff at the barn door, and into the furrow of the plow boy. Meanwhile the birds in the nest shiver and complain and call and wonder why the mother-bird does not come back. She has gone for food. After a while there is a whirr of wings and the mother-bird stands on the edge of the nest and the little ones open their mouths and the food is dropped in; and then the old bird spreads out her feathers and all is peace. Sometimes God leaves us. He goes off to get food for our soul; and then he comes back after a while to the nest, and brings us promises of his grace, and the love of God is shed abroad and we are under his wings—the broad wings of the Almighty.

They are swift wings—swift when they drop upon a foe, and swift when they come to help God's friends. The fact is you cannot get away from the care of God. "Whither shall I go from thy spirit and whither shall I flee from thy presence? If I ascend up into heaven, thou art there. If I make my bed in hell, behold! thou art there. If I take the wings of the morning, and dwell in the uttermost parts of the sea, even there thy hand shall hold me."

There are times in our lives when we must have

help immediately or perish. The grace that comes too late is no grace at all. What you want is God—now. Is it not blessed to think that God is always so quick in the rescue of his children? Swifter than a thrush's wing. Swifter than a swallow's wing, swifter than an eagle's wing are the wings of the Almighty.

Come under, ye wandering souls! Ye weary, ye troubled, ye sinning, ye dying souls! Come under the wings of the Almighty. Whoever will may come. However ragged, however wretched, however abandoned, however woebegone, there is room enough under the wings, under the broad wings of the Almighty.

Those wings under which Ruth came to trust were also strong wings. Mighty to save. Mighty to destroy. "The Lord, strong and mighty—the Lord mighty in battle! Before the stroke of that pinion a fleet is nothing. An army is nothing. A world is nothing. Our enemies may be strong. Our sorrows violent. Our sins may be great. But quicker than an eagle ever hurled down from the crags a hawk or raven will the Lord God strike back our sins and our temptations if they assault us when we are once seated on the eternal rock of his salvation. What a blessed thing it is to be defended by the strong wing of the Almighty!

I have only one more thought to present. The wings under which Ruth had come to trust were gentle wings. There is nothing softer than a feather. You have noticed, when a bird returns from flight how gently it stoops over the nest. The young birds are not afraid of having their lives tramped out by the mother-bird. And so, says the Psalmist, "He shall cover thee with his wing." O the gentleness of God!

Here fold your weary wings! This is the only safe nest. The prophet says "Though thou exalt thyself like the eagle, and set thy nest among the stars, yet will I bring thee down, saith the Lord of Hosts." Under the swift wings, under the broad wings, under the strong wings, under the gentle wings of the Almighty, find shelter until the calamities are over past. Then when you want to change nests, it will only be from the valley of earth to the heights of heaven; and instead of "the wings of a dove" for which David longed, not knowing that in the first mile of their flight they would give out, you will be conducted upward by the Lord God of Israel under whose wings Ruth the beautiful Moabitess, came to trust.

FIDELITY

Filial.—As if to disgust us with unfilial conduct, the Bible presents us the story of Micah, who stole the eleven hundred shekels from his mother, and the story of Absalom, who tried to dethrone his father. But all history is beautiful with stories of filial fidelity. Epaminondas, the warrior, found his chief delight in reciting to his parents his victories. There goes Aeneas from burning Troy, on his shoulders Anchises, his father. The Athenians punished with death any unfilial conduct. There goes beautiful Ruth escorting venerable Naomi across the desert amid the howling of the wolves and the barking of the jackals. John Lawrence, burned at the stake in Colchester, was cheered in the flames by his children who said: "O God, strengthen thy servant and keep thy promise!" And Christ in the hour of excruciation provided for his old mother. Jacob kept his resolution, "I will go and see him before I die," and a little while after we find them walking the tessellated floor of the palace, Jacob and Joseph, the prime minister and the shepherd.

Maternal.—O man! O woman! if you have pre-
served your integrity and are really Christian you
have first of all to thank God, and I think next you
have to thank your mother. The most impressive
thing in the inauguration of James A. Garfield as
President of the United States was that after he had
taken the oath of office, he turned round and in the
presence of the Supreme Court and the Senate of the
United States, kissed his old mother. If I had time
to take statistics from among you, and I could ask
what proportion of you who are Christian owe your
salvation under God to maternal fidelity, I think
about three-fourths of you would spring to your
feet. "Ha! ha!" said the soldiers of the regiment
to Charlie, one of their comrades, "what has made
the change in you? You used to like sin as well as
any of us." Pulling from his pocket his mother's
letter in which, after telling of some comforts she
had sent him, she concluded: "We are all praying
for you, Charlie, that you may be a Christian," he
said, "Boys, that's the sentence."

The trouble with Sisera's mother sitting at the
window watching for news of her son from the
battlefield, was that she had the two bad qualities
of being dissolute and being too fond of personal
adornment. She makes no anxious utterance about
the wounded in battle, about the bloodshed, about
the dying, about the dead, about the principles involved in the battle going on; a battle so important
that the stars and the freshets took part, and the
clash of swords was answered by the thunder of the
skies. What she thinks most of is the bright colors
of the wardrobe to be captured, and the needlework
she expected her son would bring home from battle.
And I am not surprised to find that Sisera fought on
the wrong side, when his mother at the window of
my text, in that awful exigency had her chief

thought on the drygoods achievement and social display. God only knows how many homes have made shipwreck on the wardrobe. And that mother who sits at the window watching for vainglorious triumph of millinery and fine colors, and domestic pageantry will after a while hear as bad news from her children out in the battle of life, as Sisera's mother heard from the struggle at Esdraelon.

THE FLOWERS

The Flowers are the Angels of the Grass.—They all have voices. When the clouds speak, they thunder; when the whirlwinds speak, they scream; when the cataracts speak, they roar; but when the flowers speak, they always whisper.

All these flowers seem to address us, saying: "God will give you apparel and food. We have no wheel with which to spin, no loom with which to weave, no sickle with which to harvest, no well sweep with which to draw water; but God slakes our thirst with the dew, and God feeds us with the bread of sunshine, and God apparels us with more than Solomonic regality. We are prophetesses of adequate wardrobe. If God so clothed us, the grass of the field, will he not clothe you, O ye of little faith?" Men and women of worldly anxieties, take this message with you. How long has God taken care of you? Quarter of the journey of life? Half of the journey of life? Can you not trust him the rest of the way? God does not promise you anything like that which the Roman Emperor had on his table at vast expense—five hundred nightingales' tongues—but he has promised to take care of you. He has promised you the necessities, not the luxuries. If God so luxuriantly clothes the grass of the field, will he not provide for you, his living and immortal children? He will. No wonder Martin

Luther always had a flower on his writing-desk for inspiration. Mongo Park, the great traveler and explorer, had his life saved by a flower. He sank down in the desert to die, but, seeing a flower nearby it suggested God's merciful care, and he got up with new courage and traveled on to safety. I said the flowers are the angels of the grass. Flowers afford a mighty symbolism of Christ, who compared himself to the ancient queen, the lily, and the modern rose, when He said, "I am the rose of sharon and lily of the valley." Redolent like one, humble like the other. Like both, appropriate for the sad who want sympathizers, and for the rejoicing who want banqueters. Hovering over the marriage ceremony like a wedding bell, or folded like a chaplet in the pulseless heart of the dead.

Flowers Mean Resurrection.—Flowers mean resurrection. Death is sad enough anyhow. Let conservatory and arboretum contribute to its alleviation. The harebell will ring the victory. The passion-flower will express the sympathy. The daffodil will kindle its lamp and illumine the darkness. The cluster of asters will be the constellation.

FORGIVENESS

Sunset.—What a pillow embroidered of all colors hath the dying day! The cradle of clouds from which the sun rises is beautiful enough but it is surpassed by the many colored mausoleum in which at evening it is buried. Sunset among the mountains? It almost takes one's breath away to recall the scene. The long shadows stretching over the plain make the glory of the departing light on the tip-top crags, and struck aslant through the foliage, the more conspicuous. Saffron and gold, purple and crimson commingled. All the castles of cloud in configuration. Burning Moscows on the sky. Hanging gardens of roses in their deepest blush! Banners of vapor, red as if from carnage, in the battle of the elements. The hunter among the Adirondacks, and the Swiss villager among the Alps know what is a sunset among the mountains. After a storm at sea the rolling grandeur into which the sun goes down to bathe at nightfall is something to make weird and splendid dreams out of for a lifetime. Paul in prison writing remembers some of the gorgeous sunsets among the mountains of Asia Minor, and how he had often seen the towers of Damascus blaze in the close of the Oriental days, and he flashes out that memory when he says: "Let not the sun go down on your wrath."

Sublime and all suggestive duty for people then, and people now. Forgiveness before sundown. He who never feels the throb of indignation is imbecile. He who can walk among the injustices of the world, inflicted upon himself and others, without flush of cheek, or flash of eye, or agitation of nature, is either in sympathy with wrong or semi-idiotic. When Ananias the high priest ordered the constables of the court-room to smite Paul in the mouth, Paul fired up and said: "God shall smite thee, thou whited wall." It all depends on what you are mad at and how long the feeling lasts whether anger is right or wrong. Life is full of exasperations. Saul with David, Korah after Moses, the Pharisees after Christ, and every one has had his pursuers, and we are swindled or belied, or misrepresented or persecuted, or in some way wronged and the danger is that healthful indignation shall become baleful spite, and that our feelings settle down into a prolonged outpouring of temper displeasing to God and ruinous to ourselves. Other things being equal, the man who preserves good temper will come out ahead. An old essayist says:

A boy in Sparta having stolen a fox, kept him under his coat and though the fox was gnawing his vitals, he submitted to it rather than expose his misdeed. Many a man with a smiling face has under his jacket an animosity that is gnawing away the strength of his body, and the integrity of his soul. Better get rid of the hidden fox as soon as possible. There are hundreds of domestic circles where that which is most needed is the spirit of forgiveness. Brothers apart, and sisters apart, and parents and children apart. Solomon says a brother offended is harder to be won over than a strong city. Are there not enough sacred memories of your childhood to bring you together? There are now domestic antipathies that seem forever to have scattered all parental memories to the four winds of heaven. The hour of sundown makes to that family no practical suggestions.

O my reader, associate the sundown with your magnanimous, out-and-out, unlimited renunciation of all hatred and forgiveness of all foes. I admit it is the most difficult of all graces to practice, and at the start you may make a complete failure, but keep on in the attempt to practice it. Shakespeare wrote ten plays before he reached Hamlet, and seventeen before he reached Merchant of Venice, and twenty-eight before he reached Macbeth. And gradually you will come from the easier grades to the most difficult. Besides that, it is not a matter of personal determination so much as the laying hold of the Almighty arm of God, who will help us to do anything we ought to do. Remember that in all personal controversies the one least to blame will have to take the first step at pacification, if it be ever effective.

God forgives with a broad sweep all faults, and all neglects, and all insults, and all wrong doing, that we may copy him with mighty success. Go, harness that sublime action of your soul to an autumnal sunset, the hour when the gate of heaven opens to let the day pass into eternities, and some of the glories escape this way through the brief opening. We talk about the Italian sunsets, and sunset amid the Apennines. But I will tell you how you may see a grander sunset than any mere lover of nature ever beheld; that is by flinging into it all your hatreds and animosities, and let the horses of fire stab them. The sublimest thing God does is the sunset. The sublimest thing you can do is forgiveness. Along the glowing banks of this coming eventide let the divine and human be concurrent.

FRIENDSHIP

The Beauty of Friendship.—I see in my text the beauty of unfaltering friendship. I suppose there were plenty of friends for Naomi while she was in prosperity; but of all her acquaintances how many were willing to trudge off with her towards Judah when she had to make that lonely journey? One— the heroine of my text. One—absolutely one. I suppose when Naomi's husband was living, and they had plenty of money, and all things went well, they had a great many callers; but I suppose that after her husband died, and her property went, and she got old and poor, she was not troubled much with callers. All the birds that sang in the bower while the sun shone have gone to their nests, now the night has fallen. Oh, these beautiful sunflowers that spread out their color in the morning hour; but they are always asleep when the sun is gone down! Job had plenty of friends when he was the richest man in Uz; but when his property went and the trials came then there were none so much pestered him as Eliphaz the Temanite, and Bildad the Shuhite, and Zophar the Naamathite. Life often seems to be a mere game, where the successful player pulls down all the other men into his own lap. Let suspicions arise about a man's character and he becomes like a bank in a panic, and all the imputations rush on him and break down in a day that character which in due time would have had strength to defend itself. There are reputations that have been half a century in building, which go down under some moral exposure, as a vast temple is consumed by the touch of a sulphurous match. A hog can uproot a century plant.

In this world so full of heartlessness and hypocrisy, how thrilling it is to find some friend as faithful in days of adversity as in days of prosperity! David has such a friend in Hushai. The Jews had such a friend in Mordecai, who never forgot their cause. Paul had such a friend in Onesiphorus, who visited him in jail. Christ had such in the Marys, who adhered to him on the cross. Naomi had such a one in Ruth who cried out: "Entreat me not to leave thee, or to return from following after thee; for whither thou goest I will go; and where thou lodgest, I will lodge; thy people shall be my people, and thy God my God; where thou diest, will I die, and there will I be buried; the Lord do so to me and more also if aught but death part thee and me."

GOD

God's Asterisk.—You often find in a book or manuscript a star calling your attention to a footnote or explanation. That star the printer calls an asterisk. But all the stars of the night-heaven are asterisks, calling your attention to God, an all-observing God. Our every nerve a divine handwriting; our every muscle a pulley divinely swung; our every bone sculptured with divine suggestiveness; our every eye a reflection of the divine eye.

God's Shadow.—It is our misfortune that we mistake God's shadow for the night. If a man come and stands between you and the sun, his shadow falls upon you. So God sometimes comes and stands between us and worldly successes and his shadow falls upon us and we think wrongly, it is night. As a father in a garden stoops down to kiss his child, the shadow of his body falls upon it; and so many of the dark misfortunes of our life are not God going away from us, but our heavenly Father stooping down to give us the kiss of His infinite love. It is the shadow of a sheltering Rock, and not of a devouring lion.

God Never Undertook a Failure.—God never undertook a failure. The Old Book which is worth all other books put together, makes it plain that God has undertaken to regulate this world by Gospel influences and if he has the power he will do what he says he will, and no one who amounts to anything will deny his power. God has said a hundred times "I will," but never once has said "I cannot." We may with our tack hammers pound away, trying to mend and improve and straighten the condition of the world and be disappointed in the result, because our arms are too weak and the hammers we wield too small; but the most defiant difficulty will flatten and disappear when God with a hammer made of summer thunderbolts strikes it, saying, "The crooked shall be made straight."

God's Hand.—The Bible often talks about God's hand. I wonder how it looks. You remember distinctly how your mother's hand looked, though thirty years ago it withered away. It was different from your father's hand. When you were to be chastised, you had rather have mother punish you than father. It did not hurt so much. And father's hand was different from mother's partly because it had outdoor toil, and partly because God intended it to be different. The knuckles were more firmly set, and the palm was calloused. But mother's hand was more delicate. There were blue veins running through the back of it. Though some of the fingers were pricked with a needle, the palm of it was soft. Oh! it was very soft. Was there ever any poultice like that to take pain out of a wound? So God's hand is a mother's hand. What it touches it heals. If it smite you it does not hurt as if it were another hand. Oh, you poor wandering soul in sin, it is not a bailiff's hand that seizes you to-day. It is not a hard hand. It is not an unsympathetic hand. It is not a cold hand. It is not an enemy's hand. No. It is a gentle hand, a loving hand, a sympathetic hand, a soft hand, a mother's hand. "As one whom his mother comforteth so will I comfort you."

God's Care.—God is not going to allow you to be overthrown. A Christian woman, very much despondent, was holding her child in her arms, and the pastor, trying to console the woman in her spiritual depression, said, "There, you will let your child drop." "Oh, no," she said, "I couldn't let the child drop." He said, "You will let the child drop." "Why," she said, "if I should drop the child here, it would dash his life out!" "Well now," said the Christian minister, "do you not think God is as good as you are? Will not God, your Father, take good care of you, as you take care of your child? God will not let you drop."

A Motherly God.—God has a mother's capacity for attending to little hurts. The father is shocked at the broken bone of the child, or at the sickness that sets the cradle on fire with fever, but it takes the mother to sympathize with all the little ailments and bruises of the child. If the child have a splinter in its hand, it wants the mother to take it out, and not the father. The father says, "Oh, that is nothing," but the mother knows it is something, and that a little hurt sometimes is to a child a very great hurt. So with God, our Mother; all our annoyances are important enough to look at and sympathize with.

God the Father.—I have no sympathy with that cast-iron theology which represents God as hard, severe, and vindicative. God is a father—kind, loving, lenient, gentle, long-suffering, patient and he flies to our immortal rescue. A wealthy lady in one of the Eastern countries was going from home for some time, and she asked her daughters for some memento to carry with her. One of the daughters brought a marble tablet, beautifully inscribed; and another daughter brought a beautiful wreath of flowers. The third daughter came, and said: "Mother, I brought neither flowers nor tablet, but here is my heart. I have inscribed it all over with your name, and wherever you go it will go with you." The mother recognized it as the best of all the mementoes. Oh, that our souls might go out toward our Father—that our hearts might be written all over with the evidences of his loving kindness, and that we might not again forsake him.

God's Patience.—God has a mother's simplicity of instruction. A father does not know how to teach a child the A B C. Men are not skillful in the primary department; but a mother has so much patience that she will tell a child for the hundredth time the difference between F and G and between I and J. Sometimes it is by blocks; sometimes by the book. She thus teaches the child, and has no awkwardness of condescension in so doing. So God, with the mother, stoops down to our infantile minds. Though we are told a thing a thousand times, and we do not understand it, our heavenly Mother goes on, line upon line, precept upon precept, here a little and there a little. God has been teaching some of us thirty years, and some of us sixty years, one word of one syllable, and we do not know it yet— f-a-i-t-h, faith. When we come to that word we stumble, we halt, we lose our place, we pronounce it wrong. Still God's patience is not exhausted. God, our Mother, puts us in the school of prosperity, and the letters are in sunshine, but we cannot spell them. God puts us in the school of adversity, and the letters are black, but we cannot spell them. If God were merely a king, he would punish us; if he were simply a father, he would whip us; but God is a mother, and so we are borne with and helped all the way through.

God's Power.—We do not have to go so far up to see the power of God in the tapestry hanging around the windows of heaven, or in the horses and chariots of fire with which the dying day departs, or to look at the mountains swinging out its sword-arm from under the mantle of darkness until it can strike with its scimiter of the lightning. I love better to study God in the shape of a fly's wing, in the formation of a fish's scale, in the snowy whiteness of a pond-lily. I love to track his footsteps in the mountain moss, and to hear his voice in the hum of the rye-fields, and discover the rustle of his robe of light in the south wind. Oh! this wonder of divine power that can build a habitation for God in an apple blossom, and tune a bee's voice until it is fit for the eternal orchestra, and can say to a firefly, "Let there be light," and from holding an ocean in the hollow of his hand, goes forth to find heights and depths and lengths and breadths of omnipotency in a dew-drop, and dismounts from a chariot of midnight hurricane to cross over on the suspension bridge of a spider's web. You may take your telescope and sway it across the heavens in order to behold the glory of God; but I will take the leaf holding the spider and the spider's web, and I will bring the microscope to my eye, and while I gaze and look and study, and am confounded, I will kneel down in the grass and cry: "Great and marvelous are thy works, Lord God Almighty."

God's Army.—It is comparatively easy to keep on a parade amid a shower of bouquets, and hand-clapping, and the whole street full of huzzas, but it is not so easy to stand up in the day of battle, the face blackened with smoke, the uniform covered with the earth plowed up by whizzing bullets, and bursting shell, half the regiment cut to pieces, and yet the commander crying: "Forward march!" Then it requires old-fashioned valor. The great trouble with the Kingdom of God in this day is the cowards. They do splendidly on a parade day, and at the communion table, when they have on their best clothes of Christian profession; but put them out in the great battle of life, at the first sharp shooting of skepticism they dodge, they fall back, they break ranks. We confront the enemy, we open the battle against fraud, and lo! we find on our side a great many people that do not pay their debts. And we open the battle against intemperance, and we find on our side a great many people who drink too much. And we open the battle against profanity and we find on our side a great many men who make hard speeches. And while we ought to be massing our troops and bringing forth more than the united courage of Austerlitz and Waterloo, and

Gettysburg, we have to be spending our time hunting up ambuscades. There are a great many in the Lord's army who like to go out on a campaign with satin slippers, and holding umbrellas over their heads to keep off the dew and having rations of canvas-back ducks. If they cannot have them they want to go home. They think it unhealthy to be among so many bullets.

God's Mercy.—Religion is always a surprise to any one that gets it. The story of grace is an old story. Apostles preached it with rattle of chain; martyrs declared it with arm of fire; deathbeds have affirmed it with visions of glory, and ministers of religion have sounded it through the lanes and the highways, and the chapels, and the cathedrals. It has been cut into stone with chisel, and spread on the canvas with pencil; and it has been recited in the doxology of great congregations. And yet when a man first comes to look on the palace of God's mercy he exclaims with prayers, with tears, with sighs, with triumph: "The half was not told me."

Religious Hope.—We want more common sense in the obtaining of religious hope. All men understand that in order to succeed in worldly directions they must concentrate. They think on that one subject until their mind takes fire with the velocity of their own thoughts. All their acumen, all their strategy, all their wisdom, all their common sense they put in that one direction, and they succeed. But how seldom it is in the matter of seeking after God! While no man expects to accomplish anything for this world without concentration, and enthusiasm, how many there are expecting afterwhile to get into the kingdom of God without the use of such means.

God's Smile.—A father and his child are walking out in the fields on a summer day and there comes up a thunder-storm. A flash of lightning startles the child, and the father says, "My dear, that is God's eye." There comes a peal of thunder and the father says, "My dear, that is God's voice." But the clouds go off the sky, and the storm is gone, and the light floods the heavens and floods the landscape, and the father forgets to say, "That is God's smile."

"God Only Can Make a Mansard."—Louis XIV, while walking in the garden at Versailles, met Mansard the architect, and the great architect took off his hat before the king. "Put on your hat," said the king, "for the evening is damp and cold." And Mansard, the architect, the rest of the evening kept on his hat. The dukes and marquises standing with bare heads before the king expressed their surprise at Mansard, but the king said: "I can make a duke or a marquis, but God only can make a Mansard." And I say to you, my hearers, only God by his convicting and converting grace can make a Christian; but he is ready this very half-hour to accomplish it.

Geysers.—The Devil's Grist mill is the name of one of the geysers of California, that group of boiling springs now famous. Indeed the whole region has been baptized with Satanic nomenclature. The guide showed us what he called the "Devil's Mush-pot," the "Devil's Pulpit," the "Devil's Machine Shop," and hearing a shrill whistle in the distance we were informed it was the "Devil's Tea-Kettle." Seeing some black water rushing from a fountain, from which the people of the neighborhood and tourists dip up genuine ink, we were told it was the "Devil's Inkstand." Indeed, you are prepared for this on the Pacific Railroad, as your

guide book points you to the "Devil's Gate," and
the "Devil's Slide," and the "Devil's Peak."

We protest against this surrender of all the geysers to the arch demon. All the writers talk of the
place as infernal. We do not believe this place so
near to hell as to heaven. We doubt if Satan ever
comes here. He knows enough of hot climates, by
experience; to fly from the hiss of these subterran-
eous furnaces. Standing amid the roaring, thundering, stupendous wonder of two hundred spouting
water springs, we felt like crying out, "Great, and
marvelous are thy works, Lord God Almighty!"

Let all the chemists and geologists of the world
come and see the footstep of God in crystals of alum
and sulphur and salt. Here is the chemist's shop
of the continent. Enough black indelible ink rushes
out of this well, with terrific splash, to supply all
the scribes of the world. There are infinite fortunes
for those who will delve for the borax, nitric and sul-
phuric acid, soda, magnesia and other valuables.
Enough sulphur here to purify the blood of the race,
or in gunpowder to kill it; enough salt to savor all
the vegetables of the world. Its acid water, which
waits only for sugar to make it delicious lemonade,
may yet be found in all the drug stores of the
country. The water in one place roars like a steamboat discharging its steam. Your boots curl with
the heat as you stand on the rot rocks, looking. Almost anywhere a thrust of your cane will evoke a
gush of steam. Our thermometer, plunged into one
spring, answered one hundred and seventy-five degrees of heat. Thrust into the "Witches Caldron"
it asserted two hundred and fifteen degrees. "The
Ink-stand" declared itself two hundred degrees.
An artificial whistle placed at the mouth of one of
these geysers may be heard miles away. You get a
hot bath without paying for it. The guide warns
you off the crust in certain places, lest you at the

same moment be drowned and boiled. Here an egg cooks hard in three minutes. The whole scene is unique and incomparable.

The geysers remind us of nothing that we ever saw or ever expect to see. They have a voice, a bubble, a smoke, a death-rattle peculiar to themselves. No photographist can picture them, no words can describe them, no fancy can sketch them.

Let us ascribe to Satan nothing that is grand, or creative, or wise. He could not make one of these grains of alum. He could not blow up one of these bubbles in the spring. If the devil wants to boil his "Tea-kettle," or stir his "Mush-pot" or whirl his "Grist mill," let him do it on his own territory. Meanwhile let the water, and the fire, and vapor praise the Lord!

HAPPINESS

Happiness Under All Circumstances.—There is a great deal of common sense in the Scriptural advice to the Hebrews: "Be content with such things as ye have." To be content is to be in good humor with our circumstances, not picking a quarrel with our obscurity, or our poverty, or our social position. The poorest of us have all that is indispensable in life.

You see people happy and miserable amid all circumstances. I stopped one day on Broadway at the head of Wall Street and the foot of Trinity Church to see who seemed the happiest people passing. I judged from their looks the happiest people were not those who went down into Wall Street, for they had on their brow the anxiety of the dollar they had lost; nor the people who swept by in splendid equipage, for they met a carriage finer than theirs. The happiest person in all that crowd, judging from the countenance was the woman who sat at the apple-stand knitting. I believe real happiness oftener looks out of the window of an humble home than through the opera-glass in the gilded box of a theater.

I find Nero growling on a throne. I find Paul singing in a dungeon. I find King Ahab going to bed at noon through melancholy, while nearby is Naboth contented in the possession of a vineyard. The wealthiest man, forty years ago, in New York when congratulated over his large estate replied, "Oh, you don't know how much trouble I have in taking care of it." Byron declared in his last hours that he had never seen more than twelve happy days in his life. I do not believe he had seen twelve minutes of thorough satisfaction. Napoleon said, "I turn in disgust from the cowardice and selfishness of man. I hold life a horror; death a repose. What I have suffered the last twenty days is beyond human comprehension."

Religion Brings Happiness.—My friends, there is no solid happiness in anything but religion. Amid the bacchanalia of Belshazzar's feast and the glittering of chalices there always will come out a handwriting on the wall, the fearfully ominous "Tekel," weighed in the balance and found wanting. When you can reap harvests off bare rocks and gather balm out of night shade, and make sunlight sleep in the heart of sepulchers, and build a firm house on a rocking billow, then an unpardoned soul can find firm enjoyment amid its transgressions.

Every Day a Triumph.—The soul's happiness is too large a craft to sail up the stream of worldly pleasure. As ship-carpenters say, it draws too much water. This earth is a bubble, and it will burst. This life is a vision, and it will soon pass away. Time! It is only a ripple, and it breaketh against the throne of Judgment. Our days! They fly more swiftly than a shuttle, weaving for us a robe of triumph or a garment of shame. Begin your life with religion and for its greatest trial you will be ready. Every day will be a triumph and death will be only a king's servant calling you to a royal banquet.

Happiness in Brute Creation.—The whole earth is filled with animal delight—joy feathered and scaled and horned and hoofed. The bee hums it; the frog croaks it; the squirrel chatters it; the quail whistles it; the lark carols it; the whale spouts it. The snail, the rhinoceros, the grizzly bear, the toad, the wasp, the spider, the shell-fish, have their homely delights—joy as great to them as our joy is to us. Goat climbing the rocks; anaconda crawling through the jungle; buffalo plunging across the prairie; crocodile basking in tropical sun; seal puffing on the ice; ostrich striding across the desert; are so many bundles of joy; they do not go moping or melancholy; they are not only half-supplied; God says they are filled with good.

The worm squirming through the sod upturned of plowshare and the ants racing up and down the hillock, are happy by day and happy by night. Take up a drop of water under the microscope and you will find that within it there are millions of creatures that swim in a hallelujah of gladness. The sounds in nature that are repulsive to our ears are often only utterances of joy—the growl, the croak, the bark, the howl. The good God made these creatures, thinks of them ever, and will not let a plowshare turn up a mole's nest, or fisherman's hook transfix a worm until, by eternal decree, its time has come. God's hand feeds all these broods and shepherds all these flocks and tends all these herds. He sweetens the clover-top for the oxen's taste; and

pours out crystalline waters, in mossed cups of rocks
for the hind to drink out of on his way down the
crags; and pours nectar into the cup of the honey-
suckle to refresh the humming-bird; and spreads a
banquet of a hundred fields of buckwheat and lets
the honey-bee put his mouth to the cup of all the
banquet; and tells the grasshopper to go anywhere
he likes and gives the flocks of heaven the choice
of all the grain-fields. The sea-anemone, half animal, half flower, clinging to the rock in mid-ocean
with its tentacles spread to catch its food, has the
Owner of the universe to provide for it. We are
repulsed at the hideousness of the elephant, but God
for the comfort and convenience of the monster,
puts forty thousand distinct muscles in its proboscis.

HEALTH

Take Care of It.—Take care of all your physical
forces, nervous, muscular, bone, brain, cellular; for
all you must be brought to judgment. The care of
your health is a positive Christian duty. Whether
we keep early or late hours, whether we shall take
food, digestible or indigestible, whether there shall
be thorough or incomplete mastication, are questions
very often deferred to the realm of whimsicality; but
the Christian man lifts this whole problem of health
into the accountable. What right has any man or
woman to deface the temple of the Holy Ghost?

What is the ear? Why, it is the whispering gallery of the human soul. What is the eye? It is
the observatory, God-constructed, its telescope
sweeping the heavens. What is the hand? An instrument so wonderful that when the Earl of
Bridgewater bequeathed in his will $40,000 for
treatises to be written on the wisdom, power, and
goodness of God, Sir Charles Bell, the great English anatomist and surgeon, found his illustration

in the construction of the human hand, devoting his whole book to that subject. So wonderful are these bodies that God names His own attributes after different parts of them. His omniscience—it is God's eye. His omnipresence—it is God's ear. His omnipotence—it is God's arm. A body so divinely honored and so divinely constructed—let us be careful how we use it.

Gospel of Health.—By the mistake of its friends religion has been chiefly associated with sick-beds and graveyards. The whole subject to many people is odorous with chlorine and carbolic acid. There are people who cannot pronounce the word religion without hearing in it the clipping chisel of the tombstone cutter. It is high time that this thing were changed, and that religion, instead of being represented as a hearse to carry the dead, should be represented as a chariot in which the living are to triumph.

Religion, so far from subtracting from one's vitality, is a glorious addition. It is sanative, curative, hygienic. It is good for the eyes, good for the ears, good for the spleen, good for the digestion, good for the nerves, good for the muscles. When David prayed that religion might be dominant, he did not speak of it as a mild sickness, or an emaciation, or an attack of moral and spiritual cramp, he spoke of it as "the saving health of all nations," while God promises longevity to the pious, saying, "With long life I will satisfy him."

Religion is sunshine; that is health. Religion is fresh air and pure water. Religion is warmth; that is healthy. Ask all the doctors and they will tell you that a quiet conscience and pleasant anticipation are hygienic. I offer you perfect peace now and hereafter. "The leaves of the tree of life for the healing of all nations." "The day-spring from on high hath visited us."

The Grandest Luxury.—We make a great ado about our hardships, but how little we talk of our blessings. Health of body, which is given in largest quantity to those who have never been petted and fondled and spoiled by fortune, we take as a matter of course. Rather have this luxury and have it alone, than without it look out of a palace window upon parks of deer stalking between fountains and statuary. People sleep sounder on a straw mattress, than fashionable invalids on a couch of ivory and eagles' down. Dinners of herbs taste better to the appetite sharpened on a woodman's ax or a reaper's scythe than wealthy indigestion experiences seated at a table covered with partridge and venison and pineapple.

The grandest luxury God ever gave a man is health. He who trades that off for all the palaces of the earth is infinitely cheated. We look back at the glory of the last Napoleon, but who would have taken his Versailles and his Tuileries if with them he had to take his gout?

HEAVEN

Exquisitely Beautiful.—I sometimes hear people representing heaven in a way that is far from attractive to me. It seems almost a vulgar heaven as they represent it with great blotches of color and bands of music making a deafening racket. John represents heaven as exquisitely beautiful. Three crystals. In one place he says: "Her light was like a precious stone, clear as a crystal!" In another place he says: "I saw a pure river from under the throne, clear as a crystal." In another place he says: "Before the throne there was a sea of glass clear as a crystal." Three crystals! John says crystal atmosphere. That means health. Balm of eternal June. What weather 'after the world's east wind! No rack of storm clouds. One breath of that air will cure the worst tubercle. Crystal light on all the leaves. Crystal light shimmering on the topaz of the temples. Crystal light tossing in the plumes of the equestrians of heaven on white horses. But "the crystal cannot equal it." John says crystal river. That means joy. Deep and ever rolling. Not one drop of the Thames, of the Hudson or the Rhine to soil it. Not one tear of human sorrow to embitter it. Crystal, the rain out of which it was made. Crystal, the bed over which it shall roll and ripple. Crystal its infinite surface. But "the crystal cannot equal it." John says crystal sea. That means multitudinously vast. Vast in rapture. Rapture vast as the sea, deep as the sea, strong as the sea, ever changing as the sea. Billows of light. Billows of beauty, blue with skies that were never clouded and green with depths that were never fathomed. Arctics and Antarctics and Mediterraneans and Atlantics and Pacifics in crystalline magnificence. Three crystals. Crystal light falling on a crystal river. Crystal river rolling into a crystal sea. But "the crystal cannot equal it."

The Password.—There will be a password at the gate of heaven. A great multitude come up and knock at the gate. The gatekeeper says, "The password." They say, "We have no password. We were great on earth and now we come to be great in heaven." A voice from within answers, "I never knew you." Another group come up to the gate of heaven and knock. The gatekeeper says, "The password." They say, "We have no password. We did a great many noble things on earth. We endowed colleges and took care of the poor." The voice from within says, "I never knew you." Another group come up to the gate of heaven and knock. The gatekeeper says, "The password." They answer, "We were wanderers from God and deserved to die; but we heard the voice of Jesus—" "Ay! ay!" says the gatekeeper, "that is the password! Lift up your heads, ye everlasting gates, and let these people come in."

Non-Exclusiveness of Heaven.—Some talk of heaven as though it were a very handsome church, where a few favored spirits would come in and sit down on finely cushioned seats all by themselves, and sing psalms to all eternity. No, no. "I saw a great multitude that no man could number standing before the throne. He that talked with me had a golden reed to measure the city, and it was twelve thousand furlongs"—that is, fifteen hundred miles in circumference. Ah! heaven is not a little colony at one corner of God's dominion, where a man's entrance depends upon what kind of clothes he has on his back, and how much money he has in his purse; but a vast empire. God grant that the light of that blessed world may shine upon us in our last moment.

Like Navy Yard Full of Old Battle Ships.— Heaven will not be a bay into which float summer yachts after a pleasuring, with gay bunting, and with embroidered sails, as fair as when they were first unfurled. Heaven will be more like a navy yard where men-of-war with masts twisted by cyclone, men-of-war with decks scorched by shell, old "Constitutions," old "Constellations" float in, discharged from service to rest forever.

The Depot of the Ages.—It is impossible to come into contact with anything grand or beautiful, whether in art or nature or religion, without being profited and elevated. We go into an art gallery and our souls come into communion with the soul of the painter, and we hear the hum of his forests and the clash of his contests, and see the cloud blossoming of the sky and the foam blossoming of the deep. On this same principle it is profitable to look off upon the landscapes which John describes—the rivers of gladness, the trees of life, the thrones of power, and the comminglings of everlasting love. I wish that to-day I could take heaven out of the list of the intangibles and make it appear to you, as it really is, the great fact of history, the depot of the ages, the grand parlor of all God's universe. The Greek orators used sometimes with one word to stir the utmost enthusiasm of their audiences. The word was "Marathon." To-day, I would stir your deepest, highest, grandest emotion with that imperial word, "Heaven!"

Dress in Heaven.—The object of dress in this world is not only to veil the body but to adorn it. The God who twisted for the brow of the morning the blue ribbons of the sky, and slippered with violeted green grass the feet of the spring morning— surely that God does not despise ornate apparel. In this world often we wear working apparel. But when our work is all done, and these hands are folded from earthly toil and the chariots are all fashioned and the temples are all finished and the mansions are all done, no more use for working-day apparel, we shall be clothed in white. In this world we often have to wear garments of mourning. Black scarf for the arm, black gloves for the hands, black veil for the face, black band for the hat. Abraham mourning for Sarah. Isaac mourning for Rebecca. Rachel mourning for her children. David mourning for Absalom. Mary mourning for Lazarus. Every second of every minute of every hour of every day a heart breaks. But our bereavements all over, our partings ended, we standing in reunion with our loved and departed ones, what more need of the black? What more need of mourning weeds? It will be white.

Honors in Heaven.—I have a strangely beautiful book containing the pictures of the medals struck by the English Government in honor of great battles; these medals pinned over the heart of the returned heroes of the army, on great occasions, the royal family present, and the royal bands playing: the Crimean medal, the Legion of Honor, the Victorian Cross, the Waterloo medal. In your first half-hour in heaven in some way you will be honored for the earthly struggles in which you won the day. Stand up before all the Royal House of heaven and receive the insignia while you are announced as victor over the droughts and freshets of the farm field, victor over the temptations of the stock exchange, victor over professional allurements, victor over domestic infelicities, victor over mechanic's shop, victor over the storehouse, victor over home worriments, victor over physical distress, victor over heredity, victor over sin and death and hell. Take the badge that celebrates those victories through our Lord Jesus Christ. Take it in the presence of all the galleried, saintly, angelic, and Divine!

False Views.—The reason that so many people never start for heaven is because they could not stand it if they got there, if it should turn out to be the rigid and formal place some people photograph it. We like to come to church but we would not want to stay here until next Christmas. We like to hear the "Hallelujah Chorus," but we would not want to hear it all the time for fifty centuries. It might be on some great occasion possibly comfortable to wear a crown of gold weighing several pounds but it would be an affliction to wear such a crown for ever. In other words, we run the descriptions of heaven into the ground, while we make that which was intended as especial and celebrative to be the exclusive employment of souls in heaven. You might as well, if asked to describe the habits of American society, describe a Decoration Day, or a Fourth of July, or an autumnal Thanksgiving, as though it were all the time that way.

Heroes and Heroines in Heaven.—How busy we will be kept in having pointed out to us the heroes and heroines that the world never fully appreciated —the yellow-fever and cholera doctors who died, not flying from their posts; the female nurses who faced pestilence in the lazarettos; the railroad engineers who stayed at their places in order to save the train though they themselves perished. Hubert Goffin, the master-miner, who landing from the bucket at the bottom of the mine, just as he heard the waters rush in, and when one jerk of the rope would have lifted him into safety, put a blind miner who wanted to go to his sick child in the bucket and then jerked the rope for him to be pulled up, crying: "Tell them the water has burst in and we are probably lost; but we will seek refuge at the other end of the right gallery;" and then giving the command to the other miners till they digged themselves so near out that the people from the outside could come to their rescue. The multitudes of men and women who got no crown on earth, we will want to see when they get their crown in heaven.

To Be a Great Surprise.—Heaven is an old story. Everybody talks about it. There is hardly a hymn in the hymn-book that does not refer to it. Children read about it in their Sabbath-school books. Aged men put on their spectacles to study it. We say it is the shelter from the storm. We call it home. We say it is the house of many mansions. We weave together all sweet, beautiful, delicate, exhilarant words, we weave them into letters, and then spell it out in rose and lily amaranth. And yet that place is going to be a surprise to the most intelligent Christian. Like the Queen of Sheba, the report has come to us from the far country, and many of us have started. It is a desert march but we urge our camels. What though our feet be blistered with the way! We are hastening to the palace. We take all our loves and hopes and Christian ambitions, as frankincense and myrrh and cassia, to the great king. We must not rest. We must not halt. The night is coming on, and it is not safe out here in the desert. Urge on the camels. I see the domes against the sky, and the houses of Lebanon, and the temples and the gardens. See the fountains dance in the sun, and gates flash as they open to let in the poor pilgrims. Send the word up to the palace that we are coming, and that we are weary of the march of the desert. But when heaven bursts upon us it will be a great surprise—Jesus on the throne, and we made like him! All our Christian friends surrounding us in glory! All our sorrows and tears and sins gone forever! The thousands of thousands, the one hundred and forty and four thousand, the great multitude that no man can number, will cry, world without end, "The half—the half was not told me!"

Explanations in Heaven.—"Eye hath not seen, nor ear heard, neither have entered into the heart of man the things which God hath prepared for them that love him." What a place of explanation it will be! I see, every day, profound mysteries of providence. There is no question we ask oftener than Why? There are hundreds of graves that need to be explained. Hospitals for the blind, the lame, asylums for the idiotic and insane, almshouses for the destitute, and a world of pain and misfortune that demand more than human solution. God will clear it up. In the light that pours from the throne, no dark mystery can live. Things now utterly inscrutable will be illumined as plainly as though the answer were written on the jasper wall or sounded in the temple anthem.

No Titles There.—It makes no difference in that silent land whether there is a plain stone above the form which the traveler pulls aside the weeds to read the name, or a tall shaft springing into heaven as though to tell their virtues to the skies. There are no titles there for great men. The Egyptian Guano which is thrown on the fields for the enrichment of the soil is the dust raked out from the sepulchres of kings and lords and mighty men. Oh, the chagrin of those men if they had ever known that in after ages of the world they would have been called Egyptian Guano. Of how much worth now is the crown of Caesar? Who bids for it? Who trembles now because Xerxes crossed the Hellespont on a bridge of boats? Who fears because Nebuchadnezzar thunders at the gates of Jerusalem? Who cares whether or not Cleopatra married Antony? Can Cromwell dissolve the English Parliament? The heart right towards God and man—The heart wrong towards God and man—is the distinction in that silent land.

HOME

Different Meanings of the Word "Home."—Ask ten different men the meaning of the word "Home," and they will give you ten different definitions. To one it means love at the hearth, it means plenty at the table, industry at the workstand, intelligence at the books, devotion at the altar. To him it means a greeting at the door, and a smile at the chair. Peace hovering like wings. Joy clapping its hands with laughter. Life a tranquil lake. Pillowed on the ripples sleep the shadows.

Ask another man what home is, and he will tell you it is want looking out of a cheerless firegrate, kneading hunger in an empty bread tray. The damp air shivering with curses. No Bible on the shelf. Children robbers and murderers in embryo. Obscene songs their lullaby. Want in the background and sin staring from the front. No Sabbath wave rolling over that doorsill. Vestibule of the pit. Shadow of infernal walls. Furnace for forging everlasting chains. Awful word! it is spelled with curses, it weeps with ruin, it chokes with woe, it sweats with the death agony of despair.

The word "Home" in one case means everything bright. The word "Home" in the other case means everything terrific.

New Ground to Plow.—Old ground must be turned up with subsoil plow, and it must be harrowed and reharrowed, and then the crop will not be as large as that of the new ground with less culture. Now, youth and childhood are new ground, and all the influences thrown over their heart and life will come up in after-life luxuriantly. Every time you have given a smile of approbation—all the good cheer of your life will come up again in the geniality of your children. And every ebullition of anger and every uncontrollable display of wrath will be fuel to their dispositions twenty or thirty or forty years from now—fuel for a bad fire a quarter of a century from this. Make your home the brightest place on earth, if you would charm your children to the high path of virtue and rectitude and religion! Do not always turn the blinds the wrong way. Let the light which puts gold on the gentian and spots the pansy pour into your dwellings. Do not expect the little feet to keep step to a Dead March. Get your point of cheerfulness from grasshopper's leap and lamb's frisk and quail's whistle, and garrulous streamlet, which, from the rock at the mountain-top clear down to the meadow ferns under the shadow of the steep, comes looking for the steepest place to leap off at, and talking just to hear itself! If all the skies over the sea, and every mountain stream went raving mad, frothing at the mouth with mad foam, and there were nothing but simoons blowing among the hills, and there were neither lark's carol nor humming-bird's trill nor waterfall's dash, but only bear's bark and panther's scream and wolf's howl, then you might well gather into your homes only the shadows. But when God has strewn the earth and heavens with beauty and gladness, let us take into our home circles all innocent hilarity, all brightness, and all good cheer. A dark home makes bad boys and bad girls, in preparation for bad men and bad women.

A Refuge.—Home is a refuge. Life is the United States army on the national road to the front, a long march with ever and anon a skirmish and a battle. At eventide we pitch our tent and stack our arms; we hang up the war cap and lay our head on the knapsack; we sleep until the morning bugle calls us to marching and action. How pleasant it is to rehearse the victories and the surprises and the attacks of the day seated by the still camp-fire of the home circle! Yea, life is a stormy sea. With shivered masts and torn sails and hulk aleak, we put into the harbor of home. Blessed harbor! there we go for repairs in the dry dock of quiet life. The candle in the window is to the toiling man the lighthouse guiding him into port. Children go forth to meet their fathers as pilots at the Narrows take the hand of ships. The door-sill of the home is the wharf where heavy life is unladen. There is the place where we may talk of what we have done without being charged with self-adulation. There is the place where we may lounge without being undignified. There is the place where we may express affection without being silly. There is the place where we may forget our annoyances and exasperations and troubles. Forlorn earth-pilgrim! no home? Then die. That is better. The grave is brighter and grander and more glorious than this world, with no tent from marchings, with no harbor from storm, with no place to rest from this scene of greed and gouge and loss and pain. God pity the man or woman who has no home!

Voyage Ended.—An old writer tells us of a ship coming from India to France. The crew was made up of French sailors who had been long from home; years gone away from their families; and as the ship came along by the coast of France the men became uncontrollable, and they skipped the deck with glee, and they pointed to the spires of the churches where they once worshiped and to the hills where they had played in boyhood. But, the writer says, when the ship came into the port, and these sailors saw the father and mother and wife and loved ones on the wharf, and heard these loved ones call them by their names, they sprang ashore and rushed up the banks into the city, and the captain had to get another crew to bring the ship to her moorings. Thus, heaven, our fatherland, will after a while be so fully in sight we can see its towers, and we can see its mansions, and we can see its hills; and as we go into port and our loved ones shall call from that shining shore and speak our names, we will spring to the beach, leaving this old ship of a world to be managed by another crew, our rough voyaging of the seas ended forever.

Everlasting Influence.—The world grows old and the stars will cease to illuminate it and the waters to refresh it and the mountains to guard it and the heavens to overspan it and its long story of sin and shame and glory and triumph will soon turn to ashes; but influences that started in the early home roll on and roll up through all eternity—blooming in all the joy, waving in all the triumph, exulting in all the sun or shrinking back into all the darkness.

Memories of Home.—Unhappy and undisciplined homes are the caldrons of great iniquity. A good home is deathless in its influence. The parents may be dead. The old homestead may have been sold and it may have gone entirely out of the possession of the family. The house itself may be torn down. The meadow brook that wound in front of it may have changed its course or entirely dried up. The long line of old-fashioned hollyhocks and the ridges and hedges of wild rose may have been graded and in place thereof, there may be now the beauties of modern gardening. The old poplar trees may have cast down their crown of verdure and they themselves may have gone in the dust. Some day you say, "I think I'll go and look at the old place." You go and look at the old place, but oh, how changed! Your eyes are full of tears all the time you are walking around the old place. But notwithstanding all the changes in that place, it is holding influence over you, and will hold influence over you until you die. The dewdrops that you dashed from the chickweed thirty years ago, when you drove the cattle to field; the fireflies that flashed in your father's house on a summer night when the evenings were too short for a candle; the tinged pebbles you gathered into your apron from the margin of the brook; the berries you strung for a necklace, and the daisies you plucked for your hair —they have all become part of the fiber of your immortal nature. You never get away from it. If you live to ninety years, you will never get away from it.

Home a Test of Character.—Home is a powerful test of Character. The disposition in public may be in gay costume, while in private it is in dishabille. As play-actors may appear in one garb on the stage and may appear in another garb behind the scenes, so private character may be very different from public character. Private character is often public character turned wrong side out. A man may receive you into his parlor as though he were a distillation of smiles, and yet his heart may be a swamp of nettles. There are business men who all day long are mild and courteous and genial and good natured in commercial life keeping back their irritability and their petulance and their discontent; but at nightfall the dam breaks, and scolding pours forth in floods and freshets. There are people who are utterly irreconcilable, who at the loss of a pencil or an article of raiment, will blow as long and sharp as a northeast storm.

The reason men do not display their bad temper in public is because they do not want to be knocked down. There are men who hide their petulance and their irritability just for the same reason that they do not let their notes go to protest. It does not pay, or for the same reason that they do not want a man in their stock company to sell his stock at less than the right price, lest it depreciate the value. As at some time the wind rises, so after a sunshiny day there may be a tempestuous night. There are people who in public act the philanthropist, who at home act the Nero, with respect to their slippers and gown.

Now the man who is affable in public and who is irritable in private is making a fradulent over-issue of stock, and he is as bad as a bank that might have four or five hundred thousand dollars of bills in circulation with no specie in the vault.

If we have not genuine grace in the family circle, all our outward and public plausibility merely springs from fear of the world or from our own selfishness. I tell you the home is a mighty test of character! What you are at home you are everywhere, whether you demonstrate it or not.

Country Boys.—All Christ's boyhood was spent in the village of Nazareth, and its surroundings. I do not believe there was one of the surrounding fifteen hills that the boy Christ did not range from bottom to top, or one cavern in their sides he did not explore, nor one species of bird flying across the tops that he could not call by name, nor one of all the species of fauna on the steeps that he had not recognized. You see it all through his sermons. If a man becomes a public speaker, in his orations or discourses you discover his early whereabouts. What a boy sees between seven and seventeen always sticks to him. When the Apostle Peter preaches, you see the fishing nets with which he had from earliest days been familiar. And when Amos delivers his prophecy you hear in it the bleating of the herds which he had in boyhood attended. And in our Lord's sermons and conversations you see all the phases of village life, and the mountainous life surrounding it.

Streaks of nature all through Christ's sermons and conversations! With those mountains of his boyhood in his memory, do you wonder that Christ, when he wanted a good pulpit made it out of a mountain—''seeing the multitudes he went up into the mountain,'' and when he wanted especial communion with God, he took James and John and Peter into ''a mountain apart.''

As this country boy of Nazareth, came forth to atone for the sins of the world, and to correct the follies of the world, and to stamp out the cruelties of the world, and to illumine the darkness of the world, and to transfigure the hemispheres! So it has been the mission of the country boys in all ages to transform and inspire and rescue. They come into our merchandise and our court rooms and our healing art and our studios and our theology. They lived in Nazareth before they lived in Jerusalem. And but for that annual influx our cities would have enervated and sickened and slain the race. Late hours and hurtful apparel and overtaxed digestive organs and crowding environments of city life would have halted the world; but valley and mountains of Nazareth have given fresh supply of health and moral invigoration to Jerusalem, and the country saves the town. From the hills of New Hampshire and the hills of Virginia and the hills of Georgia come into our national eloquence the Websters and Clays. From the cabins of the lonely country regions come into our national destinies the Andrew Jacksons and the Abraham Lincolns. From plowboy's furrow and village counter and blacksmith's forge come most of our city giants. Nearly all the Messiahs in all departments dwelt in Nazareth before they came to Jerusalem.

I send this day thanks from these cities mostly made prosperous by country boys, to farmhouse and the prairie and the mountain cabin and the obscure homesteads of north and south and east and west; to the father and mother in plain homespun, if they be still alive, or the hillocks under they sleep the long sleep. Thanks from Jerusalem to Nazareth. But alas! that the city should so often treat the country boys as of old the one from Nazareth was treated at Jerusalem! Slain not by hammers and spikes, but by instruments just as cruel. On every street of every city the crucifixion goes on. Every year of our history shows its ten thousand of the slain. Oh, how we grind them up! Under what wheels, in what mills and for what an awful grist! Let the city take better care of these boys and young men arriving from the country. They are worth saving. Let Jerusalem be careful how it treats them!

INDIVIDUALS AS FRAGMENTS

God Makes the Race in Part.—As individuals we are fragments. God makes the race in part, and then he gradually puts us together. What I lack you make up; what you lack I make up; our deficits and surpluses of character being the cogwheels in the great social mechanism. One person has the patience, another has the courage, another the placidity, another has the enthusiasm; that which is lacking in one is made up in another, or made up by all. Buffaloes in herds, grouse in broods, quail in flocks, the human race in circles. It is in this way he balances society; this conservative and that radical keeping things even. Every ship must have its mast, cutwater, taffrail, ballast. Thank God then for Princeton and Andover, for the opposites.

I have no more right to blame a man for being different from me than a driving-wheel has a right to blame the iron shaft that holds it to the center. John Wesley balances Calvin's Institutes. A cold thinker gives to Scotland the strong bones of theology; Dr. Guthrie clothes them with throbbing heart and warm flesh. The difficulty is that we are not satisfied with just the work that God has given us to do. Our usefulness and the welfare of society depend upon staying in just the place that God has put us, or intended we should occupy.

For more compactness, and that we should be more useful, we are gathered in still smaller circles in the home group. And there we have the same varieties again; brothers, sisters, husband and wife; all different in temperaments and tastes. It is fortunate that it should be so. If a husband be all impulse, the wife must be all prudence. If one sister be sanguine in her temperament, the other must be lymphatic. Mary and Martha are necessities. There will be no dinner for Christ if there be no Martha; there will be no audience for Jesus if there be no Mary.

INDOLENCE

Genius.—You must have industry of head or hand or foot or perish. Do not have the idea that you can get along in the world by genius. The curse of this country to-day is geniuses—men with large self-conceit and nothing else. The man who proposes to make his living by his wits probably has not any. I should rather be an ox, plain and plodding and useful, than to be an eagle, high-flying and good-for-nothing but to pick out the eyes of carcasses. Even in the Garden of Eden it was not safe for Adam to be idle, so God made him an horticulturist; and if the married pair had kept busy dressing the vines, they would not have been sauntering under the trees, hankering for fruit that ruined them and their posterity! Proof positive of the fact that when people do not attend to their business they get into mischief. "Go to the ant, thou sluggard; consider her ways and be wise; which, having no guide or overseer or ruler, provideth her meat in the summer and gathereth her food in the harvest." Satan is a roaring lion, and you can never destroy him by gun or pistol or sword. The weapons with which you are to beat him back are pen and type and hammer and adze and saw and pick-ax and yardstick and the weapon of honest toil. Work, work, or die.

Indolence, the Cause of Failures.—Indolence is the cause of more failures in all occupations than you have ever suspected. People are too lazy to do what they can do, and want to undertake that which they cannot do. In the drama of life they do not want to be a common soldier carrying a halberd across a stage or a falconer or a mere attendant, and so lounge about the scenes till they shall be called to be a Macready or a Junius Brutus Booth. They say, "Give me the part of Timon of Athens rather than that of Flavius, his steward." "Let me be Cymbeline, the king, rather than Pisano, the servant." After a while they, by some accident of prosperity or circumstances, get in the place for which they have no qualification. And very soon, if the man be a merchant, he is going around asking his creditors to compromise for ten cents on the dollar. Or, if a clergyman, he is making tirades against the ingratitude of churches. Or, if an attorney, by unskillful management he loses a case in which widows and orphans are robbed of their portion. Or, if a physician, he by malpractice gives his patient rapid transit from this world to the next, as the clumsy surgeon of Charles II, King of Navarre, having sewed up the feeble limbs of the king in a sheet saturated with inflammable material, and having no knife to cut the thread, took a candle to burn off the thread, and the bandages took fire and consumed the king. One incompetent friend would have made a splendid horsedoctor, but he wanted to be professor of anatomy in a university. He could have sold enough confectionery to have supported his family but he wanted to have a sugar refinery like the Havemeyers. He could have mended shoes, but he wanted to mend the Constitution of the United States. Toward the end of life these people are out of patience, out of money, out of friends, out of everything. They go to the poorhouse or keep out of it by running in debt to all the grocery and dry-goods stores that will trust them.

The Happy People are Busy People.—I see a great many Christians with doubts and perplexities, and they seem proud of them. Their entire Christian life is made up of gloom and they seem to cultivate the spirit of despondency. I will undertake to say that in nine cases out of ten spiritual despondency is a judgment of God on idleness. Who are the happy people? The busy people. Here is a wood full of summer insects. An axman goes into the wood to cut firewood. The insects do not bother him very much, and every stroke of the ax makes them fly off. But let a man go and lie down there and he is bitten and mauled and thinks it is a horrible thing to stay in the wood. Why does he not take an ax and go to work? There are thousands of Christians now in the Church who go out amid great annoyances in life—they are not perplexed, they are all the time busy; while there are others who do nothing, and they are stung and stung and covered from head to foot with the blotches of indolence and inactivity. The first thing you have to do is to go to work in the service of the Lord.

INFLUENCE

No Negative Influence.—Every man has a thousand roots and a thousand branches. His roots reach down through all the earth; his branches spread through all the heavens. He speaks with voice, with eye, with hand, with foot. His silence often is thunder, and his life is an anthem or a doxology. There is no such thing as negative influence. We are positive in the place we occupy, making the world better or worse, on the Lord's side, or on the devil's, making up reasons for our blessedness, or banishment, and we have already done a mighty work in peopling heaven or hell. I hear people tell of what they are going to do. A man who has burned down a city might as well talk of some evil that he expects to do, or a man who has saved an empire might as well talk of some good he expects to do. By the force of your evil influence you have already consumed infinite values, *or you have by the power of a right influence won whole kingdoms for God.*

A Tremendous Leverage.—I saw in some of the picture galleries of Europe, before many of the great works of the old masters, artists making copies of the pictures. These copies they were going to carry with them perhaps to distant lands, and I have thought that your life and character is a masterpiece and it is being copied, and long after you are gone it will bloom or blast in the homes of those who know you, and be Gorgon or Madonna. Look out what you say. Look out what you do. Eternity will be the echo. The best sermon is a holy life. The best music ever chanted is a consistent walk. At your feet to-day there is an influence with tremendous leverage. Your children, your children's children, and all generations that are to follow will grip that influence and feel the long reaching pull, long after the figures on your tombstones are so nearly worn out that the visitor cannot tell whether it was in 1885 or 1775 or 1675 that you died.

Personal Influence.—No one realizes how great he is for good or for evil. There are branchings out and rebounds and reverberations and elaborations of influence that cannot be estimated. The fifty or one hundred years of our earthly stay are only a small part of our sphere. The flap of the wing of the destroying angel that smote the Egyptian oppressors, the wash of the Red Sea over the heads of the drowned Egyptians were all fulfillments of promises four centuries old. And things occur in your life and in mine that we cannot account for. They may be the echoes of what was promised in the sixteenth or seventeenth century. Oh, the prolongation of the divine memory!

A Right Example.—It would be absurd for me to elaborate argument to prove the world is off track. You might as well stand at the foot of an embankment, amid the wreck of a capsized rail-train, proving by elaborate argument that something is out of order. Adam tumbled over the embankment sixty centuries ago, and the whole race in one long train has gone on tumbling in the same direction. Crash! Crash! The only question now is by what leverage can the crushed thing be lifted? By what hammer can the fragments be reconstructed?

We may help them by the charm of a right example. A man with the grace of God in his heart, and Christian cheerfulness in his face, and holy consistency in his behavior, is a perpetual sermon; and a sermon differs from others in that it has but one head, and the longer the better. There are honest men who walk down Wall Street, making the teeth of iniquity chatter. There are happy men go into a sickroom and by look help the broken bone to knit, and the excited nerves drop to calm beating. There are pure men whose presence silences the tongue of uncleanliness. The mightiest influence for good on earth is a consistent Christian. I like the Bible folded between lids of cloth or calfskin, but I like it better when in the shape of a man it goes out into the world—a Bible illustrated. Courage is beautiful to read about; but rather would I see a man with all the world against him confident as though all the world was for him. Patience is beautiful to read about; but rather would I see a buffeted soul calmly waiting for the time of deliverance. Faith is beautiful to read about; but rather would I find a man in the midnight walking straight on as though he saw everything.

The Circle.—The most beautiful figure in all geometry is the circle. God made the universe on the plan of a circle—the stars in a circle, the moon in a circle, the sun in a circle, and the throne of God is the center of that circle. While yet people thought that the world was flat and thousands of years before they found out that it was round, Isaiah intimated the shape of it, "It is He that sitteth on the circle of the earth."

There are in the natural world straight lines, angles, parallelograms, diagonals, quadrangles; but these evidently are not God's favorites. Almost everywhere where you find him geometrizing, you find the circle dominant, and if not the circle then the curve which is a circle that died young! If it had lived long enough it would have been a full orb periphery; an ellipse is a circle pressed only a little too hard at the sides. Out of a great many figures God seems to have selected the circle as the best.

The history of the world goes in a circle. The curve is in the right direction, the curve will keep right on until it becomes the circle. What is true in the material universe is true in God's moral government and spiritual arrangement. We ourselves start the circle of good or bad actions, and that will surely come around again to us unless by divine intervention it be hindered. Those good or bad actions may make the circuit of many years but come back to us they will as certainly as that God sits on the circle of the earth.

Do not be impatient because you cannot see the curve of events and therefore conclude that God's government is going to break down. History tells us that in the making of the Pyramids it took 2,000 men two years to drag one great stone from the quarry and put it into the pyramids. Well, if men short-lived can afford to work as slowly as that cannot God in the building of the eternities afford to wait? Shall we take our little watch which we have to wind up every night lest it run down and hold it up beside the clock of eternal ages? If according to the Bible a thousand years are in God's sight as one day, then according to that calculation the six thousand years of the world's existence had been only to God as from Monday to Saturday.

But it is often the case that the rebound is quicker, the return much quicker than that. The circle is sooner completed. You utter a slander against your neighbor. It has gone forth from your teeth; it will never come back, you think. You have done the man all the mischief you can. You rejoice to see him wince. That word has gone out, that slanderous word on its poisonous and blasted way. You think it will never do you any harm. But I am watching that word and I see it beginning to curve, and it curves around, and it is aiming at your heart. You had better dodge it, you cannot dodge it. It rolls into your bosom, and after it rolls in a word of an old book which says, "With what measure ye mete it shall be measured to you again."

I would like to see Paul the invalid missionary at the moment when his influence comes to full orb— I should not like to see the countenance of Voltaire when his influence comes to full orb.

Do not make the mistake of thinking that this doctrine of the circle stops with this life; it rolls on through heaven.

INSIGNIFICANCES

No Ciphers in God's Arithmetic.—Nothing with God is something. There are no ciphers in God's arithmetic. And if we were only good enough of sight, we could see as much through a microscope as through a telescope. Those things that may be impalpable and infinitesimal to us, may be pronounced and infinite to God. A mathematical point is defined as having no parts, no magnitude. It is so small you cannot imagine it, and yet a mathematical point may be a starting-point for eternity. God's surveyors carry a very long chain. A scale must be very delicate that he can weigh with it that which is so small that a grain is a million times heavier. When John Kitto, a poor boy on a back street of Plymouth, cut his foot with a piece of glass, God bound it up so successfully that Kitto became the great Christian geographer, and a commentator known among all nations. So every wound of the soul, however insignificant, God is willing to bind up.

No Insignificance in Our Lives.—There are no insignificances in our lives. The most minute thing is part of a great magnitude. Infinity is made up of infinitesimals. Great things are the aggregation of small things. Events which seem most insignificant may be momentous. That casual meeting—you did not think of it again for a long time, but how it changed every phase of your life. It seemed to be a matter of no importance that Luther found a Bible in a monastery; but as he opened that Bible and the brass-bound lids fell back, they jarred everything, from the Vatican to the furthest convent in Germany, and the rustling of the wormed leaves was the sound of the wings of the angel of the Reformation. One boat of papyrus on the Nile freighted with events for all ages. The fate of Christendom is a basket let down from a window on the wall. What you do do well. If you make a rope make it strong and true for you know not how much may depend on your workmanship. If you fashion a boat let it be waterproof for you know not who may sail in it. The casual, the accidental, that which merely happens so, are parts of a great plan, and the rope that lets the fugitive apostle from the Damascus Wall is the cable that holds to its moorings the ship of the Church in the northeast storm of the centuries.

Slip of Paper.—A poor soldier went into the store of a hair-dresser in London and asked for money to get back to the army. He had already stayed beyond his furlough, and he must have quick transit. The hair-dresser felt sorry for him and gave him the money. "Now," said the poor soldier, "I have got nothing to give you in return for your kindness except this little slip of paper, which has on it a recipe for making blacking." The man received it, not supposing it to be of any great value. But it has yielded the man who took it two million five hundred thousand dollars, and was the foundation of one of the greatest manufacturing establishments of England.

God's Construction of a Spider's Eye.—There are many Christians who are willing to serve God but they say "if we had some great occasion, if we had lived in the time of Luther, if we had been Paul's traveling companion, if we could serve God on a large scale we would do it; but we can't in everyday life." Do not think that any work God gives you to do in the world is on too small a scale for you to do it. I could show you a woman who has had rheumatism for twenty years who has endured more suffering and exhausted more grace than would have made twenty martyrs pass triumphantly through the fire. If you are not faithful in an insignificant position in life, you would not be faithful in a grand position.

When I find out that God does not forget any blossom of the spring or any snow-flake of the winter, I come to the conclusion that we can afford to attend to the minute things in life, and that what we do we ought to do well since there is as much perfection in the construction of a spider's eye as in the conformation of flaming galaxies.

Things of This World Compared With the Next.—Do not adopt the absurd preachment, that the things of this world are of little importance as compared with the next world. On the contrary, you cannot sufficiently appreciate the importance of this world, for it decides your next world. You might as well despise a schoolhouse because it is not a university. In the schoolhouse we prepare for the university. If this world is of such little importance, I do not think the first-born and the last-born of heaven would have spent thirty-three years down here to redeem it.

INTEMPERANCE

The Expensive Draught.—Lorenzo de Medici was very sick and some of his superstitious friends thought if they could dissolve a certain number of pearls in a cup and then he would drink them it would cure him of the disease. So they went around and gathered up all the beautiful pearls they could find, and they dissolved them in a cup, and the sick man drank them. It was an expensive draught. But I tell you of a more expensive draught than that. Drunkenness puts into its cup the pearl of physical health, the pearl of domestic happiness, the pearl of respectability, the pearl of Christian hope, the pearl of an everlasting heaven, and presses it to hot lips.

America's Crop of Drunkards.—America is a fruitful country, and we raise large crops of wheat and corn and oats, but the largest crop we raise in this country is the crop of drunkards. With sickle made out of the sharp edges of the broken glass of bottle and demijohn they are cut down, and there are whole swaths of them, whole windrows of them, and it takes all the hospitals and penitentiaries and graveyards and cemeteries to hold this harvest of hell.

Gladstone on Drink.—William E. Gladstone said—I think it was the first time he was Chancellor of the Exchequer—when men engaged in the ruinous traffic came to him and said their business ought to have more consideration from the fact that it paid such a large revenue to the English Government, "Gentlemen, don't worry yourselves about the revenue; give me thirty millions of sober people, and we'll have revenue enough and a surplus."

Solomon on Drink.—Are you fond of pictures? Here is one drawn by Solomon: "Who hath woe? who hath sorrow? who hath contentions? who hath babbling? who hath wounds without cause? They that tarry long at the wine; they that go to seek mixed wine. Look not thou upon the wine when it is red, when it moveth itself aright in the cup. At the last it biteth like a serpent and stingeth like an adder."

The Chain You Cannot Break.—I think if some of you should try to break away, you would find a chain on the right wrist, and on the left; one on the right foot and another on the left. This serpent does not begin to hurt until it has wound 'round and 'round. Then it begins to tighten and strangle and crush until the bones crack and the blood trickles and the eyes start from their sockets, and the mangled wretch cries, "O God! O God! help! help!" But it is too late; and not even the fires of woe can melt the chain when once it is fully fastened.

Charles Lamb on Drink.—Charles Lamb, who made all the world laugh at his humor and then afterward made all the world weep at his fate, who outwitted everybody, and was at last outwitted of his own appetites, wrote thus: "The waters have gone over me; but out of the depths, could I be heard, I would cry out to all those who have set a foot in the perilous flood. Could the youth to whom the flavor of the first wine is delicious as the opening scenes of his life, or the entering upon some newly discovered paradise—could he look into my desolation and be made to understand what a dreary thing it is when a man shall feel himself going down a precipice with open eyes and a passive will; to see his destruction and have no power to stop it, yet feel it all the way emanating from himself; to see all godliness empty out of him, and yet not able to forget that time when it was otherwise; to bear about the piteous spectacle of his own ruin—could he see my feverish eye, feverish with last night's drinking, and feverishly looking for to-night's repetition of that folly—could he but feel the body of the death out of which I cry hourly with feeble outcry to be delivered, it were enough to make him dash the sparkling beverage to the earth in all the pride of its mantling temptation.''

The Vine Bears Three Grapes.—Anacharsis said that the vine bore three grapes: the first was Pleasure, the next was Drunkenness, and the next Misery.

Drink Exhilarating.—Here is a young man who says, ''I cannot see why they make such a fuss about the intoxicating cup. Why, it is exhilarating! It makes me feel well. I can talk better, think better, feel better. I cannot see why people have such prejudice against it.'' A few years pass on, and he wakes up and finds himself in the clutches of an evil habit which he tries to break, but cannot; and he cries out, ''O Lord God! help me!'' It seems as though God would not hear his prayer; and in an agony of body and soul he cries out, ''It biteth like a serpent, and it stingeth like an adder.'' How bright it was at the start! How black it was at the last!

Deceptiveness of Strong Drink.—This subject also impresses me with the fact that fruits that are sweet to the taste may afterward produce great agony. Forbidden fruit for Eve was so pleasant she invited her husband also to take of it; but her banishment from Paradise and six thousand years of sorrow and wretchedness and war and woe paid for that luxury. Sin may be very sweet at the start, and it may induce great wretchedness afterward. The cup of sin is sparkling at the top, but there is death at the bottom. Intoxication has great exhilaration for a while, and it fillips the blood, and it makes a man see five stars where others can see only one star; and it makes the poor man think himself rich, and turns cheeks which are white red as roses; but what about the dreams that come after, when he seems falling from great heights, or is prostrated by other fancied disasters, and the perspiration stands on the forehead—the night dew of everlasting darkness—and he is ground under the horrible hoof of nightmares shrieking with lips that crackle with all-consuming torture? "Rejoice, O young man, in thy youth; and let thy heart cheer thee in the days of thy youth; but know thou that for all these things God will bring thee into judgment!"

The Perils of Intemperance.—I was told at Des Moines of a train of cars going through a very stormy night over one of the western prairies. The young man who was present told us the story. In the night there was a little child in the sleeping-car, fretful and worrying and crying hour after hour. A man on the opposite side of the car lost his patience, and said: "Either make that child shut up or take it to its mother!" Then another man on the opposite side of the sleeping-car—a man with a broken heart—pushed back the curtain and looked out and said: "Young man, that child's mother is dead in the baggage-car and the little thing is wailing for her." Then the man who had committed the affront rose up, offered his services for the night, and took care of the child until the morning, and all the passengers in the car were broken down with emotion. Oh! if the cry of one child could rouse so many sympathies, what ought to be the effect of the ten-thousand-voiced shriek of orphanage and widowhood from the inebriate's grave? God save this country from the perils of strong drink.

Must Vote Only For Sober Men.—We will grapple with this evil by voting only for sober men. How many men are there who can rise above the feelings of partisanship, and demand that our officials shall be sober men? I maintain that the question of sobriety is higher than the question of availability; and that, however eminent a man's services may be, if he have the habits of intoxication he is unfit for any office in the gift of a Christian people. Our laws will be no better than the men who make them.

KINDNESS

Lincoln's Kindness.—When Abraham Lincoln pardoned a young soldier at the request of his mother, the mother went down the stairs of the White House, saying: "They have lied about the President's being homely; he is the handsomest man I ever saw." All over that President's rugged face was written the kindness which he so well illustrated when he said: "Some of our generals complain that I impair discipline and subordination in the army by my pardons and respites, but it makes me rested after a hard day's work if I can find some good excuse for saving a man's life, and I go to bed happier as I think how joyous the signing of my name will make him and his family." Kindness! It makes the face to shine while life lasts, and after death puts a summer sunset between the still lips and the smoothed hair, that makes me say sometimes at obsequies: "She seems too beautiful to bury."

The Beauty of Kindness.—I was reading of three women who were in rivalry about the appearance of the hand. And the one reddened her hand with berries and said the beautiful tinge made her hand the most beautiful. And another put her hand in the mountain brook, and said, as the waters dripped off, that her hand was the most beautiful. And another plucked flowers off the bank and under bloom contended that her hand was the most beautiful. Then a poor old woman appeared and looking up in her decrepitude asked for alms. And a woman who had not taken part in the rivalry gave her alms. And all the women resolved to leave to this beggar the question as to which of all the hands present was the most attractive, and she said: "The most beautiful of them all is the one that gave relief to my necessities," and as she so said her wrinkles and rags and her decrepitude and her body disappeared and in its place thereof stood the Christ, who long ago said: "Inasmuch as ye did it to one of the least of these, ye did it to me!"

Kindness To a Child.—While there is life there is hope. When in England a young lady asked for a class in a Sunday-school, the superintendent said, "Better go out on the street and get your own class." She brought in a ragged and filthy boy. The superintendent gave him good apparel. In a few Sundays he absented himself. Inquiry discovered that in a street fight he had his decent apparel torn off. He was brought in and a second time respectably clad. After a few Sundays he again disappeared and it was found that he was again ragged and wretched. "Then," said the teacher, "we can do nothing with him." But the superintendent fitted him up again and started him again. After a while the Gospel took hold of him and his heart changed. He started for the ministry and became a foreign missionary and on the heathen grounds lived and translated the Scripture and preached until among the most illustrious names of the church on earth and in heaven is the name of glorious Robert Morrison. Go forth and save the lost, and remember however depraved, however raggy, however filthy and undone a child is or a man is or a woman is, they are worth an effort. I would rather have their opportunity than any that will ever be given to those who lived a magnificent sin and splendid unrighteousness and then wrapped their gorgeous tapestry around them and without a prayer expired.

Unconsciously Rescuing His Own Son.—A Bayonne merchant was in the south of Europe for his health, and sitting on the terrace one morning in his invalidism, he saw a rider flung from a horse into the river, and without thinking of his own weakness, the merchant flung off his invalid's gown and leaped into the stream and swam to the drowning man, and clutching him as he was about to go down the last time, bore him in safety to the bank, when glancing into the face of the rescued man, he cried: "My God! I have saved my own son!" All kindness comes back to us in one way or another; if not in any other way than in your own face. Kindness! Show it to others, for the time may come when you will need it yourself. People laughed at the lion, because he spared the mouse that ran over him, when by one motion of his paw, the monster could have crushed the insignificant disturber. But it was well that the lion had mercy on the mouse, for one day the lion was caught in a trap, and roared fearfully because he was held fast by ropes. Then the mouse gnawed off the ropes and let the lion go free. You may consider yourself a lion, but you cannot afford to despise a mouse.

Written On the Face.—No one could wonder at the unusual geniality in the face of William Windom, Secretary of the Treasury of the United States, after seeing him at New York banquet just before he dropped dead, turning his wineglass upside down saying, "I might by doing this offend some, but by not doing it, I might damage many." Be kind to your friends. Be kind to your enemies. Be kind to the young. Be kind to the old. Morning, noon and night be kind, and the effects of it will be written in the language of your face. That is the Gospel of physiognomy.

LIES

Many Ways of Telling a Lie.—There are thousands of ways of telling a lie. A man's whole life may be a falsehood and yet never with his lips may he falsify once. There is a way of uttering falsehood by look, by manner as well as by lip. There are persons who are guilty of dishonesty of speech and afterward say "maybe," calling it a white lie, when no lie is that color. The whitest lie ever told was as black as perdition. There are those so given to dishonesty of speech that they do not know when they are lying. With some it is an acquired sin and with others it is a natural infirmity. There are those whom you will recognize as born liars. Their whole life, from cradle to grave is filled up with vice of speech. Misrepresentation and prevarication are as natural to them as the infantile diseases, and are a sort of moral croup or spiritual scarlatina. Then there are those who in after life avail themselves of opportunities of developing this evil and they go from deception to deception, and from class to class, until they are regularly graduated liars. At times the air in our cities is filled with falsehood, and lies cluster around the mechanic's hammer, blossom on the merchant's yardstick, and sometimes sit in the door of churches. They are called by some, fabrication, and they are called by some, fiction. You might call them subterfuge or deceit or romance or fable or misrepresentation or delusion; but as I know nothing to be gained by covering up a God-defying sin with a lexicographers' blanket, I shall call them in plainest vernacular, lies. They may be divided into lies, agricultural, commercial, mechanical, social, and ecclesiastical.

Country Lies.—There is something in the presence of natural objects that has the tendency to make one pure. The trees never issue false stock. Rye and oats never move out in the night not paying for the place they occupy. Corn-shocks never make false assignment. The gold of the wheat field is never counterfeit. But while the tendency of agricultural life is to make one honest, honesty is not the characteristic of all who come to the city markets from the country districts.

The tendency of all rural districts is to suppose that sin and transgressions cluster in our great cities; but citizens and merchants long ago learned that it is not always safe to calculate from the character of the apples on the top of the farmer's barrel what is the character of the apples all the way down towards the bottom. Milk cans are not always honest. Do not let those who live in country life, come to the conclusion that all the dishonesties belong to city life.

No Such Thing as a Small Sin.—In commercial life there are those who apologize for the deviations from the right and for practical deception by saying it is commercial custom. In other words, a lie by multiplication becomes a virtue.

Who would take the responsibility of saying how many falsehoods were yesterday told by hardware men, and clothiers, and lumber men, and tobacconists, and jewelers, and importers and shippers, and dealers in furniture, and dealers in coal, and dealers in groceries? Lies about buckles, about saddles, about harness, about shoes, about hats, about coats, about shovels, about tongs, about forks, about chairs, about horses, about lands, about everything. There are social lies; society is struck through and through with insincerity. There are ecclesiastical lies, those which are told for the advancement or retarding of a church or sect.

Let us in all departments of life stand back from deception. But some one says, "The deception that I practice is so small that it amounts to nothing." It amounts to a great deal. There is no such thing as a small sin. They are all vast and stupendous, because they will all have to come under inspection in the day of judgment.

LIFE

At Hill Top.—While in early life we are climbing up the steep hillside, we have worries and frets, and we slip and fall and slide back and run upon sharp antagonisms, and all the professions and occupations have drudgeries and sharp rivalries at the start, we are afraid we will not be properly appreciated. We toil on and we pant and we struggle and we are out of breath, and sometimes we are tempted to lie down in the bower of lazy indulgence. In addition to these difficulties of climbing the hill of life, there are those who rejoice in setting a man back and trying to make a young man cowed down. Every young man has had somebody to meet him, as he was climbing up, and say to him: "Don't, don't—you can't, you can't—quit, quit!" Every

young man has had twenty disheartenments where
he has had one round word of good cheer. But after
we have climbed to the top of the hill of life, then
we have comparative tranquillity and repose. We
begin to look about us. We find that it is just
three miles from cradle to grave: Youth the first
mile, manhood the second mile, old age the third
mile. Standing on the hilltop of the journey of life
and in the second mile, having come up one side of
the hill, and before I go down the other side, I
want to tell you that life is to me a happiness, and
much of the time it has been to me a rapture, and
sometimes an ecstasy.

Sharp Curves of Life.—You stand among the
Allegheny mountains, especially near what is called
the "Horseshoe," and you will find a train of cars
almost doubling on itself, and sitting in the back
car you see a locomotive coming as you look out of
the window, and you think it is another train, when
it is only the front of the train in which you are
riding; and sometimes you can hardly tell whether
the train is going toward Pittsburg or toward
Philadelphia; but it is on the track, and it will reach
the depot for which it started, and all the passengers will be discharged at the right place. Now,
there are a great many sharp curves in life. Sometimes we seem to be going this way, and sometimes
we seem to be going that way; but if we are Christians we are on the right track and we are going
to come out at the right place.

A Reason for Congratulation.—What a thing to
congratulate you on is your life! Why, it is worth
more than all the gems of the universe kindled into
one precious stone. I am alive! What does that
mean? Why, it means that I still have all opportunity of being saved myself, and helping others to

be saved. To be alive! Why, it means that I have yet another chance to correct my past mistakes, and make sure work for heaven. Alive, are we? Come, let us celebrate it by new resolutions, new self-examination, new consecration, and a new career. The smallest and most insignificant to-day, is worth to us more than five hundred yesterdays. Taking advantage of the present let us get pardon for all the past, and security for all the future. Where are our forgiven sins? I don't know. God don't know either. He says, "Your sins and iniquities will I remember no more."

Long Life Should Be Coveted by Agnosticism.— If I were an agnostic I would say a man is blessed in proportion to the number of years he can stay on *terra firma*, because after that he falls off the docks, and if he is ever picked out of the depths it is only to be set up in some morgue of the universe to see if anybody will claim him. If I thought God made man only to last forty or fifty or a hundred years, and then he was to go into annihilation, I would say his chief business ought to be to keep alive and even in good weather to be very cautious, and to carry an umbrella and take overshoes and life preservers and bronze armor weapons of defense lest he fall off into nothingness and obliteration.

Life a Voyage in Which We Must Frequently Tack.— A sailing vessel starts from New York for Glasgow. Does it go in a straight line? Oh, no! It changes its tack every little while. Now, you say, "This vessel, instead of going to Glasgow, must be going to Havre, or it is going to Hamburg or it is going to Marseilles." No, no! It is going to Glasgow. And in this voyage of life we often have to change our tack. One storm blows us this way, and another storm blows us that way; but he who holds the winds in his fist will bring us into a haven of everlasting rest just at the right time. Do not worry, then, if you have to change tack. One of the best things that ever happened to Paul was being thrown off his horse. One of the best things that ever happened to Joseph was being thrown into the pit. The losing of his physical eyesight helped John Milton to see the battle of the angels. One of the best things that ever happened to Ignatius was being thrown to the wild beasts in the Colosseum and while eighty thousand people were jeering at his religion he walked up to the fiercest of all lions and looked him in the eye, as much as to say, "Here I am, ready to be devoured for Christ's sake."

Hot Axle.—We were on the lightning train for Cleveland. We had no time to spare. If we stopped for a half hour we should be greeted by the anathema of a lecturing committee. We felt a sort of presentiment that we should be too late, when to confirm it the whistle blew and the brakes fell, and the cry all along the train was "What is the matter?" Answer: "Hot Axle!" The wheels had been making too many revolutions in a minute. The car was on fire. It was a very difficult thing to put out; water, sand, and swabs were tried, and caused long detention, and a smoke that threatened flame down to the end of the journey.

We thought then and we think now, this is what is the matter with people everywhere. In this swift "express" American life we go too fast for endurance. We think ourselves getting on splendidly, when in the midst of our successes we come to a dead halt. What is the matter? Nerves or muscles or brains give out. We have made too many revolutions in an hour. A hot axle!

Men make the mistake of working according to

their opportunities, and not according to their capacity of endurance. "Can I run this train from Springfield to Boston at the rate of fifty miles an hour?" says an engineer. Yes. "Then I will run it reckless of consequences." "Can I be a merchant, and a president of a bank, and a director in a life insurance company, and a school commissioner, and help edit a newspaper and supervise the politics of our ward, and run for Congress?" "I can," the man says to himself. The store drives him; the school drives him; politics drive him. He takes all the scoldings and frets and exasperations of each position. Some day at the height of the business season he does not come to the most important meetings of the bank directors. In the excitements of the political canvass he fails to be at the place appointed. What is the matter? His health has broken down. The train halts long before it gets to the station. A hot axle.

Literary men have found great opportunities opening in this day. If they take all that opens, they are dead men, or worse, living men who ought to be dead. The pen runs so easily when you have good ink, and smooth paper, and an easy desk to write on and consciousness of an audience of one, two or three thousand readers. There are the religious papers through which you preach, and the musical journals through which you may sing, and the agricultural periodicals through which you can plow, and family newspapers in which you may romp with whole household around the evening lamp. There are critiques to be written, and reviews to be indulged in, and poems to be chimed, and novels to be constructed. When out of a man's pen he can shake recreation, and friendship, and usefulness, and bread he is apt to keep it shaking. So great are the invitations to literary work that the professional men of the day are overcome. They sit faint and fagged out on the verge of newspapers and books. Each one does the work of three, and these men sit up late at night and choke down chunks of meat without mastication and scold their wives through irritability and maul innocent writers and run the physical machinery with a liver miserably given out. The driving shaft has gone fifty times a second. They stop at no station. The steam-chest is hot and swollen. The brain and the digestion begin to smoke. Stop, ye flying quills! "Down brakes!" "A hot axle."

Our earthly life is a treasure to be guarded. It is an outrageous thing to die when we ought to live. There is no use in firing up a Cunarder to such a speed that the boiler bursts mid-Atlantic, when at a more moderate rate it might have reached the docks at Liverpool. It is a sin to do the work of thirty years in five years.

A Rocky Mountain locomotive engineer told us that at certain places they change locomotives and let the machine rest, as a locomotive always kept in full heat soon got out of order. Our advice to all overworked good people is "Slow up." Slacken your speed as you come to the crossings. All your faculties for work at this rate will be consumed. You are on fire now—see the premonitory smoke. A hot axle!

We need another proclamation of emancipation. The human locomotive goes too fast. Cylinder, driving-boxes, rock-shaft, truck and valve-gear need to "Slow up." Oh! that some strong hand would unloose the burdens from our over-tasked American life, that these lungs, and quenched eyes, the law, and medicine, and theology less frequently stopped in their glorious progress, because of the hot axle!

Life Starting Without a Plan.—A safeguard that I want to present to young men is a high ideal of life. Sometimes soldiers going into battle shoot into the ground instead of into the hearts of their enemies. They are apt to take aim too low, and it is very often that the captain, going into conflict with his men, will cry out: "Now, men, aim high!" The fact is that in life a great many men take no aim at all. The artist plans out his entire thought before he puts it upon canvas, before he takes up the crayon or the chisel. An architect thinks out the entire building before the workmen begin. Although everything may seem to be unorganized, that architect has in his mind every Corinthian column, every Gothic arch, every Byzantine capital. A poet thinks out the entire plot of his poem before he begins to chime the cantos of tinkling rhymes. And yet there are a great many men who start the important structure of life without knowing whether it is going to be a rude Tartar's hut or a St. Mark's Cathedral; and begin to write out the intricate poem of their life without knowing whether it is to be a Homer's Odyssey or a rhymester's botch. Out of one thousand, nine hundred and ninety-nine have no life-plot. Booted and spurred and caparisoned they hasten along and I run out and say: "Hello, man! Whither away?" "Nowhere!" they say. O young man! Make every day's duty a filling up of the great life-plan. Alas! that there should be on this sea of life so many ships that seem bound for no port. They are swept everywhither by wind and wave, up by the mountains and down by the valleys. They sail with no chart. They gaze at no star. They long for no harbor. Young man, have a high ideal and press toward it, and it will be a mighty safeguard. There were never grander opportunities opening before young men than now. Young man of the strong arm and of the stout heart and of the bounding step, I marshal you to-day for great achievement.

Life Very Precious.—Life is very precious, and if we would not give up all, there are many things we would surrender rather than surrender it. We see how precious life is from the fact that we do everything to prolong it. Hence all sanitary regulations, all study of hygiene, all fear of draughts, all doctors, all medicines, all struggle in crisis of accident. An admiral of the navy was court-martialed for turning his ship around in time of danger, and so damaging the ship. It was proved against him. But when his case came to be heard he said: "Gentlemen, I did turn the ship around and admit that it was damaged, but do you want to know why I turned it? There was a man overboard, and I wanted to save him, and I did save him, and I consider the life of one sailor worth all the vessels of the British navy." No wonder he was vindicated. Life is very precious.

Life With or Without God.—Are you going to undertake the work of life with nothing but your own brain or arm, or with your own brain and arm backed up by all the terrestrial and all the celestial forces of the Almighty? I offer you God! He tells me to make that point-blank proposition. If you want them you can have them on your side for the earnest asking—Omniscience, Omnipresence, Omnipotence! Can you imagine a greater contrast than a young man undertaking life alone—life with all its confrontments of temptation and obstacle—and a young man undertaking life with every wing of angel and every thunderbolt of heaven pledged for his defense and advancement; the difference between a young man alone, and a young man befriended by the Maker and Upholder of the Universe? The battle of life is so severe that no young man can afford to decline any help, and the mightiest help is God. One night in the year 1741 Count

Lessock went to escort the Princess Elizabeth of
Russia to a throne which was then unoccupied. She
halted, she hesitated, she wondered whether she had
better go to the palace and mount the throne of all
the Russias. Then Count Lessock drew on a paper
two sketches, the one of herself and the Count in
disgrace and on the scaffold, and the other of herself on a throne amid acclaiming subjects. When
she saw plainly that she must make a choice, she
chose the throne. I put before the young men of
America the choice between overthrow and en-
thronement. You may have what you will. Will
you be the slave to passion and sin and death, or
a conqueror empalaced? The Spanish proverb was
right when it said, "The road of By and By leads
to the town of Never."

The Purpose of Life.—By the time a child reaches
ten years of age the parents begin to discover the
child's destiny; but by the time he or she reaches
fifteen years of age the question is on the child's
lips: "What am I to be? What am I going to do?"
It is a sensible and righteous question, and the youth
ought to keep on asking it until it is so fully answered that the young man or the young woman can
say with as much truth as its author, though on a
less expansive scale: "To this end was I born."

Games of Life.—We never get over being girls,
and boys. The good healthy man of sixty years
of age is only a boy with added experience. A
woman only an old girl. Summer is but an older
spring. August is May in its teens. We shall be
useful in proportion as we keep young in our feelings. There is no use for fossils except in museums
and on the shelf. I like young old folks.

Indeed we keep doing over what we did in childhood. You thought that long ago you got through

with "blind-man's buff" and "hide-and-seek" and "Puss-in-the-corner" and "Tick-Tack-Toe" and "leap-frog" but all our lives are passed in playing those games over again.

Much of our time we go about blindfolded, stumbling over mistakes, trying to catch things we miss, while people stand round the ring and titter, and break out with half-suppressed laughter and push us ahead, and twitch the corner of our eye-bandage. After a while we vehemently clutch something with both hands, and announce to the world our capture; the blindfold is taken from our eyes, and amid shouts of the surrounding spectators, we find we after all caught the wrong thing. What is that but "blind-man's buff" over again?

The funniest play I ever joined in at school, and one that makes me laugh now as I think of it is "Leap-frog." It is inartistic and homely. It is so humiliating to the boy who bends himself over and puts his hands on his knees, and it is so perilous to the boy who placing his hands on the stooped shoulders attempts to fly over. But I always preferred the risk of the one who attempted the leap, rather than the humiliation of the one who consented to be vaulted over. It was often the case that we both failed in our part and we went down together. For this Jack Snider carried a grudge against me and would not speak, because he said I pushed him down a-purpose. But I hope he has forgiven me by this time, for he has been sent out as a missionary. Indeed, if Jack will come this way I will right the wrong of olden time by stooping down in my study and letting him spring over me as my children do.

Almost every Autumn I see that old-time school feat repeated. Mr. So-and-So says, "You make me governor and I will see that you are assessor. You stoop down and let me jump over you and then I will stoop down and let you jump over me. Elect me deacon and you shall be trustee. You write a good thing about me and I will write a good thing about you." The day of election in church and State arrives. A man once very upright begins to bend. You cannot understand it, he goes down lower and lower until he gets his hands away down on his knees. Then a spry politician or ecclesiastic comes up behind him and puts his hand on the bowed strategist and springs clear over into some great position. Good thing to have a good man in a prominent position. Good thing to have a good man in a prominent place. But after a while he himself begins to bend. Everybody says, "What is the matter now? It cannot be possible he is going down too." Oh yes! Turn about is fair play. One half the strange things in Church and State may be accounted for by the fact that ever since Adam bowed down so low as to let the race, putting its hands on him, fly over into ruin, there has been a universal and perpetual tendency to political and ecclesiastical "leap frog."

In one sense, life is a great "game of ball." We all choose sides and gather into denominational and political parties. We take our places on the ball ground. Some are to pitch; they are the radicals. Some are to catch; they are the conservatives. Some are to strike; they are those fond of politics and parties. Some are to run; they are the candidates. There are four bases—youth, manhood, old age and death. Some one takes the bat, lifts it and strikes for the prize and misses it, while the man who was behind catches it and goes in. This man takes his turn at the bat, sees the flying ball of success, takes good aim, and strikes it high amid the clappings of all the spectators. We all have a chance at the ball. Some of us run to all four bases, from youth to manhood, from manhood to old age, from old age to death. At the first base we bound with uncontrolled mirth; coming to the second, we run with slower but stronger tread; coming to the third, our step is feeble; coming to the fourth, our breath entirely gives out. We throw down the bat on the black base of death, and in the evening catchers and pitchers go home to find the family gathered. So may we all find the candles lighted and the table set, and the old folks at home.

MAN

World Adapted to Man's Happiness.—Notice the adaptation of the world to the comfort and happiness of man. The sixth day of creation had arrived. The palace of the world was made, but there was no king to live in it. Leviathan ruled the deep; the eagle of the air; the lion of the field; but where was the scepter which should rule all? A new style of being was created. Heaven and earth were represented in his nature. His body from the earth beneath; his soul from the heaven above. The one reminding him of his origin, the other speaking of his destiny—himself the connecting link between the animal creation and angelic intelligence. In him a strange commingling of the temporal and eternal, the finite and the infinite, dust and glory. The earth for his floor, and heaven for his roof; God for his Father; eternity for his lifetime. So quietly and mysteriously does the human body perform its functions, that it was not until five thousand years after the creation of the race that the circulation of the blood was discovered; and though anatomists of all countries and ages have been so long exploring this castle of life, they have begun to understand it.

Volumes have been written on the hand. Wondrous instrument! With it we give friendly recognition and grasp the sword and climb the rock and write and carve and build. It constructed the Pyramids and hoisted the Parthenon. In it the white marble of Pentelicon mines dreamed itself away into immortal sculpture. It reins in the swift engine; it holds the steamer to its path in the sea; it snatches the fire from heaven; it feels the pulse of the sick; and makes the nations quake with its stupendous achievements. What power brought down the forests and made the marshes blossom and burdeneth the earth with all the cities that thundered on with enterprise and power?

Behold the eye, which in its Daguerrean gallery, in an instant catches the mountain and the sea. This perpetual telegraphing of the nerves; these joints that are the only hinges that do not wear out; this furnace, whose heat is kept up from the cradle to grave; this factory of life, whose wheels and spindles and bands are God-directed; this human voice, capable, as has been estimated, of producing millions of different sounds. If we could realize the wonders of our physical organization, we would be hypochondriacs, fearing every moment that some part of the machine would break down.

Look at man's mental constitution. Behold the lavish benevolence of God in powers of perception. Watch the law of association, or the mysterious linking together of all you ever thought of, knew or felt, and then giving you the power to take hold of the clew-line and draw through your mind the long train with indescribable velocity—one thought starting up a hundred, and this again a thousand—as the chirp of one bird sometimes wakes a whole forest of voices. Watch your memory—the sheaf-binder that goes forth to gather the harvest of the past and bring it into the present. Your power and velocity of thought—thought of the swift wing and the lightning foot.

In reason and understanding, man is alone. The ox surpasses him in strength, the antelope in speed, the hound in keenness of nostril, the eagle in far-reaching sight, the rabbit in quickness of hearing, the honey-bee in delicacy of tongue, the spider in fineness of touch. Man's power, therefore, consists not in what he can lift or how fast he can run or how strong a wrestler he can throw—for in these respects the ox, the ostrich, and the bear are his superior—but by reason he comes forth to rule all; through his ingenious contrivance to outrun, outlift, outwrestle, outsee, outhear, outdo.

Responsibility of Men of Power.—It is a stupendous thing to have power—political power, social power, official power. It has often been printed and often quoted as one of the wise sayings of the ancients, "Knowledge is power." Yet it may as certainly be power for evil as good. The lightning express rail-train has power for good, if it is on the track, but horrible power for disaster if it leaves the track and plunges down the embankment. The ocean steamer has power for good, sailing in right direction and in safe waters and under good helmsman and wide-awake watchman on the lookout, but indescribable power for evil if under full headway it strikes the breakers. As steam-power or electricity or water forces may be stored in boilers, in dynamos, in reservoirs, to be employed all over town or city; so God sometimes puts in one man enough faith to supply thousands of men with courage. If a man happens to be thus endowed, let him realize his opportunity and improve it.

Good Men Cannot be Killed.—You may assault a good man, but you cannot kill him. On the day of his death, Stephen spoke before a few people in the Sanhedrin; this Sabbath morning he addresses all Christendom. Paul, the Apostle, stood on Mars Hill addressing a handful of philosophers who knew not so much about science as a modern school-girl. To-day he talks to all the millions of Christendom about the wonders of justification and the glories of resurrection. John Wesley was howled down by a mob to whom he preached, and they threw bricks at him, and they denounced him and they jostled him, and they spat upon him, and yet to-day, in all lands, he is admitted to be the great father of Methodism. Booth's bullet vacated the great presidential chair; but from that spot of coagulated blood on the floor in the box of Ford's Theater, there sprang up the new life of a nation.

Wise for This World—Fools for Eternity.—There are many who are wise for this world, and who are fools for eternity. Some astronomers with their telescopes sweep the heavens, yet are not able to see the morning star of the Redeemer. Many a man acquainted with the higher branches of mathematics is not able to do a plain sum in the Gospel arithmetic: "What shall it profit a man if he gain the whole world and lose his soul?" Men able to botanize across the Rose of Sharon and the Lily of the Valley.

Obstreperous People.—Passing along a country road quite recently, we found a man, a horse, and wagon in trouble. The vehicle was slight, and the road was good, but the horse refused to draw and his driver was in a bad predicament. He had already destroyed his whip in applying inducements to progress in travel. He had pulled the horse's ears with a sharp string. He had backed into the ditch. He had built a fire of straw underneath him, the only result a smashed dash board. The chief effect of the violence and cruelties applied was to increase the divergency of feeling between the brute and master. We said to the besweated and outraged actor in the scene that the best thing for him to do was to let his horse stand for a while unwhipped and uncoaxed, leaving some one to watch him while he, the driver went away to cool off. We learned that the plan worked admirably; that the cool air and the appetite for oats, and the solitude of the road favorable for contemplation, had made the horse move for adjournment to some other place and time; and when the driver came up, he had but to take up the reins and the beast erst so obstinate dashed down the road at a perilous speed.

There is not so much difference between horses and men as you might suppose. The road between mind and equine instinct is short and soon traveled. The horse is sometimes superior to his rider. If anything is good and admirable in proportion as it answers the end of its being, then the horse that bends into its traces before the truck is better than its blaspheming driver. He who cannot manage a horse cannot manage men.

We know of pastors who have balky parishioners. When any important move is to take place, and all the other horses of the team are willing to draw, they lay themselves back in the harness. First the pastor pats the obstreperous elder or deacon on the neck and tells him how much he thinks of him. This only makes him shake his mane and grind his bit. He will die first before he consents to such a movement. Next he is pulled by the ear, with a good many insinuations as to his motives for holding back. Fires of indignation are built under him for the purpose of consuming his balkiness. He is whipped with the scourge of public opinion, but this only makes him kick fiercely and lie harder in the breeching-straps. He is backed down into the ditch of scorn and contempt, but still is not willing to draw an ounce. O foolish minister, trying in that way to manage a balky parishioner! Let him alone. Go on and leave him there. Pay less attention to the horse that balks, and give more oats to those that pull. Leave him out in the cold. Some day you will come back and find him glad to start.

At your first advance he will arch his neck, paw his hoof, bend to the bit, stiffen the traces and dash on. We have the same prescription for balky horses and men: for a little while let them alone.

Christian More of a Man.—When a man becomes a Christian he becomes not less than a man but more than a man. Yonder is a factory with a thousand wheels, but it is low water. Now only fifty of the thousand wheels are in motion, but after a while the spring freshets come, and the floods roll down and now all the thousand wheels have bands on them and are in motion. Before a man becomes a Christian only part of his nature is in activity and employment. The grace of God comes in with powerful floods of mercy and new impetus to action, and now instead of fifty faculties or the fifty wheels, there are a thousand all in play and in full motion.

MASTER OF THE SITUATION

Self-control.—If you would master the situation, when angry, do not utter a word or write a letter, but before you speak a word or write a word, sing a verse of some hymn, in a tune arranged in minor key and having no staccato passages. If very angry sing two verses. If in a positive rage, sing three verses. First of all the unhealthiest thing on earth is to get mad. It jangles the nerves, enlarges the spleen, and sets the heart into wild thumping. Many a man and many a woman has in time of such mental and physical agitation dropped dead. Not only that, but it makes enemies out of friends, and makes enemies more virulent, and anger is partial or consummate suicide. Great attorneys, understanding this, have often won their cause by willfully throwing the opposing counsel into a rage. There is one man you must manage or one woman you must control, in order to please God and make life a success and that is yourself. There are drawbridges to every castle by which you may keep out of your nature foreign foes, but no man has a defense against himself, unless it be a divine defense. Out of the millions of the human race there is only one person who can do you permanent and everlasting harm, and that is the being that walks under your own hat and in your own shoes.

The hardest realm that you will ever have to govern is the realm between your scalp and heel. The most dangerous cargo a ship can carry is dynamite and the most perilous thing in one's nature is an explosive temper. If your nature is hopelessly irascible and tempestuous, then dramatize placidity. If a ship is on fire, and you cannot extinguish the flames, at any rate keep down the hatches. When some injustice is inflicted upon you, or some insult offered you, or some wrong done, the best thing for you to say is to say nothing, and the best thing for you to write is to write nothing; if the meanness done you is unbearable or you must express yourself or die, then I commend a plan that I have once or twice successfully adopted. Take a sheet of paper. Date it at your home or office. Then put the wrong-doer's name at the head of the letter-page without any prefix of "Colonel" or suffix of "D.D." and begin with no term of courtesy but a bold and abrupt "Sir." Then follow it with a statement of the wrong he has done you, and of the indignation you have felt. Put into it the strongest terms of execration you can employ without being profane. Sign your name to the red-hot epistle. Fold it. Envelope it. Direct it plainly to the man who has done you wrong. Carry the letter a week or two weeks, if need be and then destroy it. In God's name destroy it! I like what Abraham Lincoln said to one of his cabinet officers. That cabinet officer had been belied and misrepresented until, in a fury, he wrote a letter of arraignment to his enemy, and in tersest possible phraseology told him what he thought of him. The cabinet officer read it to Mr. Lincoln, and asked him how he liked it. Mr. Lincoln replied, "It is splendid for sarcasm and scorn. I never heard anything more complete in that direction. But do you think you can afford to send it?" That calm and wise and Christian interrogation of the President stopped the letter, and it was never sent. Young man, before you get far in life, unless you are an exception among men, you will be wronged, you will be misinterpreted, you will be outraged. All your sense of justice will be in conflagration. Let me know how you meet that first great offense and I will tell you whether your life is to be a triumph or a failure. You see, equipoise at such a time means so many things. It means self-control. It means capacity to foresee results. It means confidence in your own integrity. It means a faith in the Lord God to see you through.

Conquering Self.—Sir Edward Creasy wrote a book called "The Fifteen Decisive Battles of the World from Marathon to Waterloo." But the most decisive battle that you will ever fight and the greatest victory you will ever gain is this moment when you conquer yourself, and then all the hindering myrmidons of perdition by saying, "Lord Jesus, here I am undone and helpless, to be saved by thee and thee alone." That makes panic in hell. That makes celebration in heaven.

Canine Philosophy.—Nick the Newfoundland lies

sprawled on the mat. He has a jaw set with strength; an eye mild, but indicative of the fact that he does not want too many familiarities from strangers; a nostril large enough to smell a wild duck across the meadows; knows how to shake hands, and can talk with head and ear, and tail; and, save an unreasonable antipathy to cats is perfect, and always goes with me on my walk out of town.

He knows more than a great many people. Never do we walk, but the poodles, and rat-terriers, and the grizzly curs with stringy hair and damp nose, get after him. They tumble off the front door step and out of the kennels, and assault him front and rear. I have several times said to him (not loud enough for the Presbytery to hear), "Nick, why do you stand all this? Go at them!" He never takes my advice. He lets them bark and snap, and passes on unprovoked without sniff or growl. He seems to say: "They are not worth minding. Let them bark. It pleases them and don't hurt me. I started out for a six-mile tramp, and I cannot be diverted. Newfoundlanders like me have a mission. My father pulled three drowning men to the beach, and my uncle on my mother's side saved a child from the snow. If you have anything brave, or good, or great for me to do, just clap your hand and point out the work, and I will do it, but I cannot waste my time on rat-terriers."

If Nick had put that in doggerel, I think it would have read well. It was wise enough to become the dogma of a school. Men and women are more easily diverted from the straight course than is Nick. Mythology represents Cerberus a monster dog at the mouth of hell, but he has had a long line of puppies. They start out as editors, teachers, philanthropists, and Christians. If these men go right on their way, they perform their mission and get their reward, but one-half of them stop and make attempts to silence the literary, political, and ecclesiastical curs that snap at them.

Many an author has got a drop of ink in his eye, and collapsed. The critic who had lobsters for supper the night before snarled at the book, and the time that the author might have spent in new work he squanders in gunning the critics.

You might have better gone straight ahead, Nick! You come to be estimated for exactly what you are worth. If a fool, no amount of newspaper or magazine puffery can set you up; if you are useful, no amount of newspaper or magazine detraction can keep you down.

For every position there are twenty aspirants; only one man can get it; forthwith the other nineteen are on the offensive. People are silly enough to think that they can build themselves up with the bricks they pull out of your wall. Pass on and leave them. What a waste of powder for a hunter to go into the woods to shoot flies, or for a man of great work to notice infinitesimal assault! My Newfoundland would scorn to be seen making a drive at a black-and-tan terrier.

But one day on my walk with Nick we had an awful time. We were coming in at great speed, much of the time on a brisk run, my mind full of white clover tops, and the balm that exudes from the woods in full leafage, when passing the commons, we saw a dog fight in which there mingled a Newfoundland as Nick, a bloodhound and a pointer. They had been inter-locked for some time in terrific combat. They had gnashed upon and torn each other until there was getting to be a great scarcity of ears, and eyes and tails.

Nick's head was up, but I advised him that he had better keep out of that canine misunderstanding. But he gave one look as much as to say, "Here at last is an occasion worthy of me," and at that dashed into the fray. There had been no order in the fight before, but as Nick entered they all pitched into him. They took him fore, and aft, and midships. It was a greater undertaking than he had anticipated. He shook, and bit, and hauled, and howled. He wanted to get out of the fight, but found that more difficult than to get in.

If there is anything I like, it is fair play. I said "Count me in!" and with stick and other missiles I came in like Blücher at night fall. Nick saw me and plucked up courage, and we gave it to them right and left, till our opponents went scampering down the hill, and I laid down the weapons of conflict and resumed my profession as a minister, and gave the mortified dog some good advice on keeping out of scrapes, which homily had its proper effect, for with head down and penitent look, he jogged back with me to the city.

Lesson for men and dogs. Keep out of fights. You will have enough battles of your own, without getting a loan of conflicts at twenty per cent a month.

Every time since the unfortunate struggle I have described, when Nick and I take a country walk and pass a dog fight he comes up close to my side, and looks me in the eyes with one long wipe of the tongue over his chops, as much as to say, "Easier to get into a fight than to get out of it. Better jog along our own way;" and then I preach him a short sermon from Proverbs 26.17: "He that passeth by, and meddleth with strife belonging not to him, is like one that taketh a dog by the ears."

MOTHER

The Unselfishness of a Mother's Love.—There is no emotion so completely unselfish as maternal affection. Conjugal love expects the return of many kindnesses and attentions. Filial love expects parental care, or is helped by the memory of past watchfulness. But the strength of a mother's love is entirely independent of the past and the future, and is of all the emotions the purest. The child has done nothing in the past to earn kindness, and in the future it may grow up to maltreat its parent; but still from the mother's heart there goes forth inconsumable affection. Abuse cannot offend it; neglect cannot chill it; time cannot affect it; death cannot destroy it. For harsh words it has gentle chiding; for a blow it has beneficent ministry; for neglect it has increasing watchfulness. It weeps at the prison door over the incarcerated prodigal, and pleads for pardon at the Governor's feet, and is forced away by compassionate friends from witnessing the struggles of the gallows. Other lights go out, but this burns on without extinguishment, as in gloom-struck night you may see a single star, one of God's pickets with gleaming bayonet of light guarding the outposts of heaven.

Mothers' Influence.—The only way you can tell the force of a current is by sailing up-stream; or the force of an ocean wave, by running the ship against it. Running along with it we cannot appreciate the force. In estimating maternal influence we generally run along with it down the stream of time, and so we do not understand the full force. Let us come up to it from the eternity side, after it has been working on for centuries, and see all the good it has done and all the evil it has accomplished multiplied in magnificent appalling compound interest. The difference between that mother's influence on her children, now, and the influence when it has been multiplied in hundreds of thousands of lives, is the difference between the Mississippi River, way up at the top of the continent, starting from the little

Lake Itasca, seven miles long and one wide, and its mouth at the Gulf of Mexico, where navies might ride. Between the birth of that river and its burial in the sea, the Missouri pours in, and the Red and White and Yazoo Rivers pour in, and all the States and Territories between the Alleghany and Rocky Mountains make contributions. Now, in order to test the power of a mother's influence, we need to come in off the ocean of eternity, and sail up toward the one cradle, and we find ten thousand tributaries of influence pouring in and pouring down. But it is, after all, one great river of power rolling on and rolling forever. Who can fathom it? Who can bridge it? Who can stop it? Had not mothers better be intensifying their prayers? Had they not better be elevating by their example? Had they not better be rousing themselves with the consideration that by their faithfulness or neglect they are starting an influence which will be stupendous after the last mountain of earth is flat, and the last sea has dried up, and the last flake of the ashes of a consumed world shall have been blown away, and all the telescopes of other worlds, directed to the track around which our world once swung, shall discover not so much as a cinder of the burned-down and swept-off planet.

Cropping Out in Succeeding Generations.—Good or bad influence may skip one generation or two generations, but it will be sure to land in the third or fourth generation, just as the Ten Commandments, speaking of the visitation of God on families, says nothing about the second generation, but entirely skips the second and speaks of the third and fourth generations: "Visiting the iniquities of the fathers upon the third and fourth generations of them that hate me." Parental influence, right or wrong, may jump over a generation but it will come down further on, as sure as you sit there and I stand here.

Appreciate a Mother's Love.—Oh, appreciate a mother's love. If heretofore you have been negligent of such a one, and you have still opportunity for reparation, make haste. If you could only look in for an hour's visit to her you would rouse up in the aged one a whole world of blissful memories. What if she does sit without talking much; she watched you for months when you knew not how to talk at all. What if she has ailments to tell about; during fifteen years you ran to her with every little scratch and bruise, and she doctored your little finger as carefully as a surgeon would bind the worst fracture. You say she is childish now; I wonder if she ever saw you when you were childish. You have no patience to walk with her on the street; she moves so slowly. I wonder if she remembers the time when you were glad enough to go slowly. Do not begrudge what you do for her. I care not how much you do for her, she has done more for you.

You will miss her when she is gone. I would give the house over my head to see my mother. I have so many things I would like to tell her, things that have happened in the twenty-four years since she went away. Morning, noon and night let us thank God for the good influences that have come down to us from good mothers.

Care of Mother.—Some of us remember when the Central America was coming home from California she was wrecked. President Arthur's father-in-law was the heroic captain of that ship, and went down with most of the passengers. Some got off into the lifeboats, but there was a young man returning from California who had a bag of gold in his hand; and as the last boat shoved off from the ship that was to go down that young man shouted to a comrade in the boat, "Here, John, catch this gold; there are three thousand dollars; take it home to my old mother, it will make her comfortable in her last days."

Mothers of Girls.—I declare to you I believe I am uttering the first word that has been uttered in appreciation of the self-denial, of the fatigues, and good sense, and prayers which those mothers go through who navigate a family of girls from the edge of the cradle to the school door, and from the school house door up to the marriage altar. That is an achievement which the eternal God celebrates high up in the heavens, though for it human hands so seldom clap the faintest applause. What a time that mother had with those girls, if she had relaxed care and work and advice and solicitation of heavenly help, the next generation would have suffered. It is while she is living, but never after she is dead that some girls call their mother "Maternal ancestor" or "the old woman." It is the almost overwhelming testimony of young women who have lost their mothers that they did not realize what she was to them until she was gone. Indeed, mother in the appreciation of many a young lady is a hindrance. The maternal inspection is often considered an obstacle. Mother has so many notions about that which is proper and which is improper. It is astonishing how much more girls know at eighteen than their mothers at forty-five. With what elaborate argument, perhaps spiced with some temper the youngling tries to reverse the opinion of the oldling. The sprinkle of gray on the maternal forehead is rather an indication to the recent graduate from boarding school that the circumstances of to-day or to-night are not fully appreciated. What a wise boarding school that would be if the mothers were the pupils and the daughters the teachers. How well the teens would chaperone the fifties. Then mothers do not amount to much, anyhow they are in the way, for mothers have such unprecedented means of knowing everything. It would take whole libraries to hold the wisdom which the daughter knows more than her mother. And the question in many a group has been, although not plainly stated, "What shall we do with the mothers anyhow? They are so far behind the times."

Permit me to suggest that if the mother had given more time to looking after herself and less time to looking after you she would have been as fully up-to-date as you in music, in style of date, in esthetic taste, and in all sorts of information. I expect that while you were studying botany and chemistry and embroidery and the new opera, she was studying household economies. Young woman, you will never have a more disinterested friend than your mother, when she says anything is unsafe or imprudent. When she declares it is something you ought to do—I think you had better do it. She has seen more of the world than you have. Do you think she could have any mercenary or contemptible motive in what she advises you to do? She would give her life for you if it were called for. Do you know any one else who would do as much? Again and again she has already endangered that life during the six weeks' diphtheria or scarlet fever and she never once brought up the question of whether she had better stay, breathing day and night the contagion. The graveyards are full of mothers who died taking care of their children. The world makes applaudatory ado over the work of mothers who have raised boys to be great men and I could turn to my bookshelves and find the names of fifty distinguished men who had great mothers. But who praises mothers for what they do for daughters who make the homes of

America? I do not know of an instance of such recognition.

God's Harmonies.—I suppose that even the sounds in nature that are discordant and repulsive make harmony in God's ear. You know you can come so near to an orchestra that the sounds are painful instead of pleasurable, and I think we stand so near devastating storm and frightful whirlwind we cannot hear that which makes to God's ear, and the ear of the spirits above us, a music as complete as it is tremendous. The day of Judgment, which will be a day of uproar and tumult, I suppose, will bring no dissonance to the ear of those who can calmly listen. That last day when the grand march will be played by the fingers of thunders and earthquake, and conflagration.

Not only is inanimate nature full of music but God has wonderfully organized the human voice, so that in the plainest throat and lungs there are fourteen direct muscles which can make over sixteen thousand different sounds! Now, there are thirty indirect muscles which can make, it has been estimated, more than one hundred and seventy million sounds. When God has so constructed the human voice, and when he has filled the whole earth with harmony, and when he recognized it in the ancient temple, I have a right to come to the conclusion that God loves music.

Music Born in Heaven.—Grand old Haydn, sick and worn out, was carried for the last time into the music hall and there he heard his own oratorio of the "Creation." History says that as the orchestra came to that famous passage, "Let there be light!" the whole audience rose and cheered, and Haydn waved his hand toward heaven and said: "It comes from there." Overwhelmed with his own music, he was carried out in his chair, and as he came to the door he spread his hand toward the orchestra as in benediction. Haydn was right when he waved his hand toward heaven and said, "It comes from there." Music was born in heaven, and it will ever have its highest throne in heaven.

God's Stringed and Wind Instruments.—There has been much discussion as to where music was born. I think that at the beginning when the morning stars sang together, and all the sons of God shouted for joy, that the earth heard the echo.

Inanimate nature is full of God's stringed and wind instruments. Silence itself—perfect silence is only a musical rest in God's great anthem of worship. Wind among the leaves, insect humming in the summer air, the rush of billow upon beach, the ocean far out sounding its everlasting psalm, the bobolink on the edge of the forest, the quail whistling up from the grass, are music.

Exclusiveness of Music.—You know that in a great many churches, the choir is expected to do all the singing, and the great mass of people are expected to be silent, and if you utter your voice you are interfering. There they stand, the four singing, "Rock of Ages cleft for me," with the same spirit with which the night before they took their parts in the "Grand Duchess" or "Don Giovanni." Have we a right to delegate to others the discharge of this duty which God demands of us? Suppose that four wood-thrushes should propose to do all the singing some bright day when the woods are ringing with bird voices. It is decided that four wood-thrushes shall do all the singing of the forest. Let all other voices keep silent. How beautifully the four warble. It is really fine music. But how long will you keep the forest still? Why, Christ would come into that forest and look up as he looked through the olive trees and he would wave his hand and say: "Let everything that hath breath praise the Lord;" and, keeping time with the stroke of innumerable wings, there would be five thousand bird voices leaping into the harmony.

Music of the Skies.—Across the harsh discords of this world rolls the music of the skies—music that breaks from the lips, music that breaks from the harps and rustles from the palms, music like falling water over rocks, music like wandering winds among leaves, music like carolling birds among forests, music like ocean billows storming the Atlantic beach: "They shall hunger no more, neither thirst any more, neither shall the sun light on them nor any heat; for the Lamb which is in the midst of the throne shall lead them to living fountains of water, and God shall wipe away all tears from their eyes."

Music in Battle.—When Napoleon was in battle and found a favorite regiment falling back he said: "What is the matter with that regiment? It is made up of some of our bravest men," and the word came to him that the brass band had stopped playing. Then he called up the fifers and pointed out to them the music, turning over the portfolio, and said, play that, and they played it; and the retreating regiment fell into line, rallied their courage and won the day. O ye who are falling back into temptations and sorrows and annoyances and exasperations of this life, just try the power of music to rally your scattered battalions.

Music Commanded by God.—God commanded music. Through Paul he tells us to admonish one another in psalms, and hymns, and spiritual songs; and through David he cried out: "Sing ye to God, all ye kingdoms of the earth." And there are scores of other passages I might name, providing that it is as much a man's duty to sing as it is his duty to pray. Indeed, I think there are more commands in the Bible to sing than there are to pray. God not only asks for the human voice but for instruments of music. He asks for the cymbal, and the harp, and the trumpet: and all the instruments of music whether they have been in the service of righteousness, or sin, will be brought by their masters and laid down at the feet of Christ, and then sounded in the church's triumph, on her way from suffering unto glory. "Praise ye the Lord!" Praise him with your voices. Praise him with stringed instruments and with organs.

Music the Praise of the Church of Christ.—David no more certainly owned the harp with which he sounded the praises of God than the Church of Christ now owns all chants, all anthems, all ivory key-boards, all organ diapasons; and God will gather up these sweet sounds after a while, and he will mingle them in one great harmony, and the Mendelssohns and the Beethovens and the Mozarts of the earth will join their voices and their musical instruments and soft south wind and loud-lunged Euroclydon will sweep the great organ pipes, and you shall see God's hand striking the keys, and God's foot trampling the pedals in the great oratorio of the ages!

Music Soothes Perturbation.—I have also noticed the power of sacred song to soothe perturbation. You have read in the Bible of Saul and how he was sad and angry and how the boy David came in and played the evil spirit out of him. A Spanish king was melancholy. The windows were all closed. He sat in the darkness. Nothing could bring him forth until Faraneli came and discoursed music for three or four days to him. On the fourth day he looked up, and wept, and rejoiced, and the windows were thrown open, and that which all the splendors of the court could not do, the power of song accomplished. If you have anxieties and worriments, try this heavenly charm upon them. Do not sit down on the bank of the hymn, but plunge in, that the devil of care may be brought out of you.

Music at the Start.—Among the first things created was the bird. Why? Because God wanted the world to have music at the start. And this infant world, wrapped in swaddling clothes of light, so beautifully serenaded at the start is to die amid the ringing blast of the archangel's trumpet; so that as the world had music at the start, it is going to have music at the last.

NAME

Keeping Family Names Bright.—Let young men beware, lest they by their behavior blot such family records with some misdeed. We can all think of households, the names of which meant everything honorable and consecrated for a long while, but by the deed of one son humiliated, disgraced and blasted. Look out how you rob your consecrated ancestry of the name they handed to you unsullied! Better, as trustee to that name, add something worthy. Do something to honor the old homestead, whether a mountain cabin or a city mansion, or a country parsonage! Rev. David Dudley Field, though thirty-two years passed upward, is honored to-day by the Christian life, the service, the death of his son Stephen.

Handicap of Name.—Many people are under the disadvantage of an unfortunate name given them by parents who thought they were doing a good thing. It is outrageous to afflict children with an undesirable name because it happened to be possessed by a parent or a rich uncle from whom favors are expected, or some prominent man of the day who may end his life in disgrace. Sometimes at the baptism of children, while I have held up one hand in prayer, I have held up the other in amazement that the parents should have weighed the babe with such a dissonant and repulsive nomenclature. I have not so much wondered that some children should cry out at the Christening font, as that others with such smiling faces should take a title that will be a burden of their lifetime. It is no excuse because they are Scriptural names to call a child Jehoikim or Tiglath. I baptized one by the name of Bathsheba. Why under all the circumambient heaven, any parent should want to give a child the name of that loose creature of Scripture times I cannot imagine. I have often felt at the baptismal altar when names were announced somewhat like saying, as did the Rev. Dr. Richards, of Morristown, New Jersey, when a child was handed to him for baptism, and the name given, "Hadn't you better call it something else?" Impose not upon that babe a name suggestive of flippancy or meanness. There is no excuse for such assault and battery on the cradle when our language is opulent with names musical and suggestive in meaning such as John, meaning "the gracious gift of God"; or Henry, meaning "the chief of a household"; or Alfred, meaning "good counselor"; or Joshua, meaning "God our salvation"; or Ambrose, meaning "immortal"; or Andrew, meaning "manly"; or Esther, meaning "star"; or Abigail, meaning "my father's joy"; or Anna, meaning "grace"; or Victoria, meaning "victory"; or Rosalie, meaning "beautiful as a rose"; or Margaret, meaning "a pearl"; or Ida, meaning "godlike"; or Clara, meaning "illustrious"; or Amelia, meaning "busy"; or Bertha, meaning "beautiful," and hundreds of other names just as good that are a help rather than a hindrance.

Disgracing the Family Name.—A reckless or dissipated son makes a heavy-hearted parent because it hurts the family pride. It is not the given name or the name which you received at the christening, that is injured by your prodigality. You cannot hurt the name of John or George or Henry or Mary or Francis because there have been thousands of people, good and bad, having those names, and you cannot improve or depreciate the respectability of those given names. But it is your last name, your family name that is at your mercy. All who bear that name are bound before God and man not to damage its happy significance. You are charged by all the generations of the past and all the generations to come to do your share for the protection and honor and the integrity of that name. You have no right, my friend, by a bad life to blot the old family Bible containing the story of the marriage and births and deaths of the years gone by or to cast a blot upon the family Bibles whose records are yet to be opened. There are in our American-city directories names that always suggest commercial dishonesty or libertinism or cruelty or meanness just because one man or woman bearing that name cursed it forever by miscreancy. Look out how you stab the family name! It is especially dear to your mother. She was not born with that name. She was born under another name, but the years passed on and she came to young womanhood, and she saw some one with whom she could trust her happiness, her life and her immortal destiny; and she took his name, took it while the orange blossoms were filling the air with fragrance, took it with joined hands, took it while the heavens witnessed. She took it out of all the family names since the world stood, for better, for worse, through sickness and through health, by cradles and by graves. Yes, she put off her old family name to take her part to make it an honorable name. How heavy a trouble you put upon her when by misdeeds you wrench that name from its high significance! To haul it down from your mother's forehead and trample it in the dust would be criminal. Your father's name may not be a distinguished name, but I hope it stands for something good. It may not be famous like that of Homer, the father of epic poetry, or Izaak Walton, the father of angling, or Æschylus, the father of tragedy, or Ethelwold, the father of monks, or Herodotus, the father of history, or Thomas Aquinas, the father of moral philosophy, or Abraham, the father of the faithful, but your father has a name in a small circle as precious to him as theirs in a larger circle. Look out how you tarnish it!

The Inebriate suffers From the Loss of a Good Name.—God has so arranged it that no man loses his reputation except by his own act. The world and all the powers of darkness may assault a man —they cannot capture him so long as his heart is pure and his life is pure. All the powers of earth and hell cannot take that Gibraltar. If a man is right, all the bombardment of the world for five, ten, twenty, forty years will only strengthen him in his position. So that all you have to do is to keep yourself right. Never mind the world. Let it say what it will. It can do you no damage. But as soon as it is whispered "he drinks," and it can be proved, he begins to go down. What clerk can get a position with such a reputation? What store wants him? What church of God wants him for a member? What dying man wants him for an executor? "He drinks!" I stand before hundreds of young men who have their reputation as their only capital. A good name. Your father gave you a good education, or as good an education as he could afford to give you. He could furnish you no means, but he surrounded you with Christian influences and a good memory of the past. Now, young man, under God you are with your own right arm to achieve your fortune, and as your reputation is your only capital, do not bring upon it suspicion by drinking liquor, or by an odor of your breath, or by any glare of your eye, or by any unnatural flush on your cheeks. You lose your reputation and you lose your capital.

NON-APPRECIATION

One of the Trials of Life.—Non-appreciation is one of the trials of life. That is what made Martha so vexed at Mary. The younger sister had no estimate of elder sister's fatigues.

Men who are bothered with the anxieties of the store, the office and shop, or who come from the stock-exchange say when they reach home: "Oh, you ought to be in our factory, a little while; you should try to manage eight or ten, or twenty subordinates, and then you would know what trouble and anxiety are!" They do not appreciate the fact that the wife and mother has to conduct at the same time a university, a clothing establishment, a restaurant, a laundry, a library, while she is a health officer, police and president of her realm. She must do a thousand things, and do them well in order to keep things going smoothly; and so her brain and her nerves are taxed to the utmost. I

know there are housekeepers who are so fortunate
that they can sit in an armchair in the library, or
lie on the belated pillow, and throw all the care
upon subordinates, who having large wages and
great experience, can attend to all of the affairs of
the household. Those are the exceptions. I am
writing of the great mass of housekeepers—the
women to whom life is a struggle, and who at thirty
years of age look as if they were forty, and at forty
look as though they were fifty, and at fifty look as
if they were sixty. The fallen at Chalons, and
Austerlitz, and Gettysburg, and Waterloo are a
small number compared with the slain in the great
Armageddon of the kitchen. You think, oh, man
of the world, that you have all the cares and anxieties. If the cares and anxieties of the household
should come upon you for one week you would be
fit for an insane asylum. The half-rested house-
keeper arises in the morning. She must have the
morning repast prepared at an irrevocable hour.
What if the fire will not light—what if the market-
ing did not come—what if the clock has stopped?
No matter; she must have the morning repast at
an irrevocable hour. Then the children must be
got off to school. What if their garments are torn?
What if they do not know their lessons? What if
they have lost their hat or sash? They must be
ready. Then she has all the diet of the day, and
perhaps for several days to plan. But what if the
butcher has sent meat unmasticable, or the grocer
has sent articles of food adulterated? and what if
some pieces of silver be gone, or some favorite
chalice be cracked, or the roof leak, or the plumber
fail, or any one of a thousand things occur? She
must be ready. Spring comes and there must be
a revolution in the family wardrobe; or autumn
comes and she must shut out the northern blasts.
But what if the moth has preceded her to the chest:

What if, during the year, the children have outgrown the apparel of last year? What if the fashions have changed? Her house must be an apothecary's shop; it must be a dispensary; there must be medicines for all sorts of ailments—something to loosen the croup, something to cool the burn, something to poultice the inflammation, something to silence the jumping tooth, something to soothe the earache. She must be in half a dozen places at the same time, or she must attempt to be. Oh, woman, though I may fail to stir up an appreciation in the souls of others in regard to your household toils, let me assure you that from the kindliness with which Jesus Christ met Martha that he appreciates you.

OPPORTUNITY

What Is an Opportunity?—What is an opportunity? The lexicon would coolly tell you it is a conjunction of favorable circumstances for accomplishing a purpose; but words cannot tell what it is. Take a thousand years to manufacture a definition and you could not successfully describe it. Opportunity! The measuring rod with which the Angel of the Apocalypse measured heaven could not measure this pivotal word. Stand on the edge of the precipice of all time and let down the fathoming line hand under hand and lower down and lower down and for a quintillion of years let it sink, and the lead will not strike bottom.

It is very swift in its motions. Sometimes within one minute it starts from the throne of God, sweeps around the earth and reascends to the throne from which it started. Within less than sixty seconds it fulfilled its mission.

Opportunity never comes back. Perhaps an opportunity very much like it may arrive, but that one never. Naturalists tell us of insects which are born, fulfill their mission, and expire in an hour; but many opportunities die so soon after they are born that their brevity of life is incalculable. What most amazes me is that opportunities do such overshadowing, far-reaching and tremendous work in such short earthly allowance.

Like a Flock of Birds.—An opportunity passed the thousandth part of a second has by one leap reached the other side of a great eternity. In the autumn when the birds migrate you look up and see the sky black with wings and the flocks stretching out into many leagues of air, and so to-day I look up and see two large wings in full sweep. They are the wings of the flying year. That is followed by a flock of three hundred and sixty-five and they are the flying days. Each of the flying days is followed by twenty-four, and they are the flying hours, and each of these is followed by sixty, and these are the flying minutes. Where did this great flock start from? Eternity past. Where are they bound? Eternity to come. You might as well go a-gunning for the quails that whistled last year in the meadows, or the robins that last year caroled in the sky, as to try to fetch down and bag one of the opportunities of your life.

One of the Loveliest and Awfulest Words In Our Language.—At Denver, Colorado, years ago, an audience had assembled for divine worship. The pastor of the church for whom I was to preach that night, interested in the seating of the people, stood in the pulpit looking from side to side, and when no more people could be crowded within the walls, he turned to me and said, with startling emphasis: "What an opportunity!" Immediately that word began to enlarge, and while a hymn was being sung, at every stanza the word "opportunity" swiftly and mightily unfolded, and while the opening prayer was being made, the word piled up into Alps and Himalayas of meaning and spread out into other latitudes and longitudes of significance until it became hemispheric, and it still grew in altitude and circumference until it encircled other worlds, and swept out and on and around until it was a big eternity. Never since have I read or heard that word without being thrilled with its magnitude and momentum. Opportunity! Although to some it may seem a mild and quiet note, in the great Gospel harmony it is a staccato passage. It is one of the loveliest and awfullest words in our language of more than one hundred thousand words of English vocabulary. "As we have opportunity let us do good."

Statue of Opportunity.—In a sculptor's studio stood a figure of the god Opportunity. The sculptor had made the hair fall down over the face of the statue so as to completely cover it, and there were wings to the feet. When asked why he so represented Opportunity, the sculptor answered, "The face of the statue is thus covered up because we do not recognize Opportunity when it comes, and the wings to the feet show that Opportunity is swiftly gone."

No Posthumous Opportunity.—There is a hovering in the minds of a vast multitude that there will be an opportunity in the next world to correct the mistakes of this; that, if we do make complete shipwreck of our earthly life, it will be on a shore up which we may walk to a palace; that, as a defendant may lose his case in the Circuit Court and carry it up to the Supreme Court, or Court of Chancery, and get a reversal of judgment in his behalf, all the costs being thrown over on the other party, so if we fail in the earthly trial, we may in the higher jurisdiction of eternity have the judgment of the lower court set aside, all the costs remitted and we be victorious defendants forever.

Improve Your Opportunity.—The day I left our country home to look after myself, we rode across the country, and my father was driving. Of course I said nothing that implied how I felt. But there are hundreds of men who from their own experience know how I felt. At such a time a young man may be hopeful, and even impatient, to get into the battle of life for himself, but to leave the homestead where everything has been done for you; your father or older brothers taking your part when you were imposed upon; and when you got a cold, your mother always around, with mustard applications for the chest, or herb tea to make you sweat off the fever, and sweet mixtures in the cup by the bed to stop the cough, taking sometimes too much of it because it was pleasant to take; and then to go out with no one to stand between you and the world, gives one a choking sensation at the throat, and a homesickness before you have got three miles away from the old folks. There was on the day I speak of, a silence for a long while, and then my father began to tell how good the Lord had been to him, in sickness and in health, and when times of hardship came how Providence had always provided the means of livelihood for the large household, and he wound up by saying, "DeWitt, I have always found it safe to trust the Lord." My father has been dead thirty years, but in the crises of my life—and there have been many of them—I have felt the mighty impetus of the lesson in the farm wagon: "DeWitt, I have always found it safe to trust the

Lord." The fact was, my father saw that it was his opportunity, and he improved it.

In the Home.—I wonder if all the heads of families realize that the opportunity of influencing the households for Christ and heaven is very brief, and will soon be gone? For a while the house is full of voices and footsteps of children. You sometimes feel that you can hardly stand the racket. And it is a rushing this way, and a rushing that, until father and mother are well-nigh beside themselves. It is astonishing how much noise five or six children make and not half try. But the years glide away. After a while the voices are not so many and those which stay are more sedate. First this room gets quiet, and then that room. Death takes some, and marriage takes others, until after a while the house is awfully quiet. That man would give all he is worth to have that boy who is gone away forever rush into the room once more with a shout that was once thought too boisterous. That mother who was once tired because her little girl, now gone forever, with careless scissors cut up something really valuable, would like to have the child come back, willing to put in her hands the most valuable wardrobe to cut as she pleased. Yes! Yes! The house noisy now will soon be still enough, I warrant you, and so when you begin housekeeping, there were just two of you, there will be just two again. Oh, the alarming brevity of infancy and childhood! The opportunity is glorious, but it soon passes. Parents may say at the close of life: "What a pity we did not do more for the religious welfare of our children while we had them with us!" But the lamentation will be of no avail. The opportunity had wings, and vanished.

Things of This World Transitory.—Do not build so much on the transitory differences of this world, for soon it will make no difference to us whether we had ten million dollars, or just ten cents, and the ashes into which the tongue of Demosthenes dissolved are just like the ashes into which the tongue of the veriest stammerer went.

Spiked Nettles of Life Part of Discipline.—Let us remember that the spiked nettles of life are part of our discipline. Life would be nauseating if it were all honey. That table would be poorly set that had on it nothing but treacle. We need a little vinegar, mustard, pepper and horse-radish that brings the tears even when we do not feel pathetic. If this world were all smoothness, we would never be ready for emigration to a higher and better. Blustering March and weeping April prepare us for shining May. This world is a poor hitching post. Instead of tying fast on the cold mountains, we had better whip up and hasten on toward the warm inn where our good friends are looking out and watching to see us come up.

The Grand March of the Union.—I have sometimes thought it might need a foreign invasion to make us forget all our sectional strife—I mean entirely and forever forget it. If such an invasion should ever come, you would see the North, the South, the East, the West, side by side as though there had never been a quarrel. I see them, in imagination, going to the conflict: Fifteenth New York volunteers, Tenth Alabama cavalry, Fourteenth Pennsylvania riflemen, Tenth Massachusetts artillery, Seventh South Carolina sharpshooters, and such a strong conjunction of officers. I do not know but it may require the attack of some foreign foe to make us forget our absurd sectional wrangling. I have no faith in the cry, "No North, no South, no East, no West." Let all four sections keep their peculiarities and their preferences, each doing its own work and not interfering with each other, each of the four carrying its part in the great harmony —the bass, the alto, the tenor, the soprano—in the grand march of the Union.

Nothing in the World Can Keep a Good Man Down.—God has decreed for him a certain elevation to which he must attain. He will bring him through though it cost Him a thousand worlds. There are constantly men in trouble lest they shall not be appreciated. Every man comes in the end to be valued at just what he is.

Take Good Aim.—It is very important to take good aim. God knows, and we know, that a great deal of Christian attack amounts to nothing simply because we do not take good aim. Nobody knows, and we do not know ourselves, which point we want to take, when we ought to make up our minds what God will have us to do, and point our spear in that direction and then hurl our body, mind, soul, time, eternity at that one target.

Faults Through Microscope, Virtues Through Telescope.—You are not the first man who had his faults looked at through a microscope, and his virtues through the wrong end of a telescope. Pharaoh had the chief butler and baker endungeoned, and tradition says that all the butler had done was to leave a gravel in the king's bread. The world has the habit of making a great ado about what you do wrong and forgetting what you do right. What a soft pillow to die on if when we leave this world we can feel that though a thousand people may have wronged us, we have wronged no one; or having made envious and jealous attacks, we have repented of the sin and as far as possible made reparation.

The King's Gallery.—Why covet the gratification of the artistic and intellectual taste when you have the original from which pictures are copied? What is a sunset on a wall compared with a sunset hung in loops of gold in the heavens? What is a cascade silent on a canvas compared with a cascade that makes the mountain tremble, its spray ascending like the departed spirit of the water slain on the rocks? Oh, there is a great deal of hollow affectation about the fondness for pictures on the part of those who never appreciate the original from which the pictures are taken. As though the parent should have no regard for a child but go into ecstasies over its photograph. Bless the Lord to-day, O man, O woman! that though you may be shut out from the works of a Rubens, and a Raphael, you still have a free access to a gallery grander than the Louvre, or Luxemburg, or Vatican, the royal gallery of the noonday heavens, the King's gallery of the midnight sky.

PATRIOTISM

Why We Should Be Patriots.—There are three great reasons why you and I should do our best for this country—three great reasons: Our fathers' graves, our cradle, our children's birthright. When I say your fathers' graves, your pulses run quickly. Whether they sleep in city cemetery or country graveyard, their dust is very precious to you. I think they lived well and that they died right. Never submit to have any government over their tombs other than that government under which they lived and died. And then this country is our cradle. It may have rocked us very roughly, but it was a good cradle to be rocked in. Oh, how much we owe to it! Our boyhood and girlhood, it was spent in this blessed country. I never have any patience with a man who talks against this country. Glorious place to be born in, and a glorious place to live in. It has been our cradle. Ay, it is to be our children's birthright. You and I will soon be through. We will perhaps see a few more spring blossoms, and we will perhaps see a few more autumnal fruits; but we are to hand this government to our children as it was handed to us—a free land, a happy land, a Christian land. They are not to be trampled by despotism. They are not to be frightened by anarchies. We must hand this government to them over the ballot-box, over the school desk, over the church altar, as we have received it, and charge them solemnly to put their life between it and any keen stroke that would destroy it.

And thou, Lord God Almighty! We put with a thousand-armed prayer, into thy protection this nation. Remember our fathers' bleeding feet at Valley Forge. Remember Marion and Kosciusko. Remember the cold, and the hunger, and the long march, and the fever hospital. Remember the fearful charge up Bunker Hill. Remember Lexington, and Yorktown, and King's Mountain, and Gettysburg. Remember Washington's prayer by the camp-fire. Remember Plymouth Rock and the landing amid the savages. Remember Independence Hall and how much it cost our fathers to sign their names. Remember all the blood and tears of three wars—1776, 1812, 1862. And more than all, remember the groan that was mightier than all other groans, and the thirst that was worse than all other thirsts, and the death that was ghastlier than all other deaths, the Mount on which Jesus died to make all men happy and free. For the sake of all this human and divine sacrifice, O God protect this nation! And whosoever would blot it out, and whosoever would strike it down, and whosoever would turn his back, let him be accursed.

PATIENCE

Remember the Corallines.—Nothing so impresses me as the fact that our Lord loves the beautiful. Sunsets and sunrises he hangs up for nations to look at; he may green the grass and round the dew into pearl, and set autumnal foliage to please mortal sight, but the thousand miles of coral achievement I think he built for his own delight. The snow of that white, and the bloom of that crimson, he alone can see; only here and there God allows specimens of submarine glory to be brought up and set before us for sublime contemplation.

The first thing that strikes me in looking at the coral is its long-continued accumulation. It is an outputting and an outbranching of ages. You sometimes get discouraged because the uplifting of the soul does not go on more quickly. The little annoyances of life are the zoöphyte builders, and there will be small layer on top of small layer and fossilized grief on fossilized grief. On forever, up forever. Out of the sea of earthly disquietude will gradually rise the reefs, the continents, the hemispheres of grandeur and glory. Men talk as if they had only in this life to build. But what we build in this life compared to what we shall build in the next life is as a striped shell to all Australia. You do not scold the corallines because they cannot build an island in a day. More slowly and marvelously accumulative is the grace in the soul than anything I can think of.

Lord help us to learn that which most of us are

deficient in, patience. If it can take the sea-anem-
ones millions of years to build one bank of coral,
ought we not be willing to do work through ten, or
fifty years without complaining, without restless-
ness, without chafing of spirit? Patience with the
erring; patience that we cannot have the millennium in a few weeks; patience at what seems slow
fulfillment of the Bible promises; patience with
physical ailment; patience under delays of Providence. Grand, glorious, all-enduring, all-conquer-
ing patience. Without it life is an irritation, but
with it life is a triumph. Patience, the sweetest
sugar for the sourest cup, the balance wheel for all
mental and moral machine. The foot that treads
into placidity the stormiest lake; the bridle for the
otherwise rash tongues; the sublime silence that
conquers the boisterous and blatant. Under all
exasperations employ it. Whatever comes, stand
it; hold on, wait, bear up. Remember the Corallines.

Thorns in the Flesh.—The Christian world has
long been guessing what Paul's thorn in the flesh
was. I have a book that in ten pages tries to show
what Paul's thorn was not, and in another ten pages
tries to show what it was.

Many of the theological doctors have felt Paul's
pulse to see what was the matter with him. I suppose that the reason he did not tell us what it was
may have been because he did not want us to know,
suffice to say, it was a thorn—that it stuck him. It
was sharp.

Every one has a thorn sticking him. The house-
keeper finds it in unfaithful domestics; or an inmate
who keeps things disordered; or a house too small
for convenience or too large to be kept cleanly.
The professional man finds it in perpetual inter-
ruptions or calls for "more copy."

One man has a rheumatic joint which when the wind is north-east, lifts the storm signal. Another a business partner who takes full half the profits, but does not help earn them. These trials are the more nettlesome because like Paul's thorn they are not to be mentioned. Men get sympathy for broken bones, but not the end of sharp thorns that have been broken off in the fingers.

Let us start out with the idea that we must have annoyances. It seems to take a certain number of them to keep us humble, wakeful and prayerful. To Paul the thorn was as disciplinary as the shipwreck. If it is not one thing it is another.

If the pen is good the ink is poor. If the editorial column be able, there must be a typographical blunder. If the thorn does not pierce the knee, it must take you in the back. Life must have sharp things in it. We cannot make up our robe of Christian character without pins and needles.

We want what Paul got—grace to bear these things. Without it we become cross, censorious and irascible. We get in the habit of sticking our thorns into other people's fingers. But God helping us, we place these annoyances in the category of the "all things that work together for good." We see how much shorter these thorns are than the spikes that struck through the palm of Christ's hands; and remembering that he had on his head a whole crown of thorns, we take to ourselves the consolation that if we suffer with him on earth we shall be glorified with him in heaven.

PERSEVERANCE

Courage to Persist.—Audubon, the great ornithologist, with gun and pencil, went through the forests of America to bring down and so sketch the beautiful birds, and after years of toil and exposure completed his manuscript and put it in a trunk in Philadelphia for a few days of recreation and rest, and came back and found that the rats had utterly destroyed the manuscript; but without any discomposure and without any fret or bad temper, he again picked up his gun and pencil and visited again all the great forests of America and reproduced his immortal work. And yet there are people with a ten-thousandth part of that loss who are utterly irreconcilable, who, at the loss of a pencil or an article of raiment, will blow as long and sharp as a northeast storm.

Endure the Scoffing.—It was very hard for Noah to endure the scoffing of the people of his day while he was trying to build the ark, and was every morning quizzed about his old boat that would never be of any practical use; but when the deluge came and the top of the mountains disappeared like the backs of sea monsters and the elements lashed up in fury, clapped their hands over a drowned world, then Noah in the ark rejoiced in his own safety and the safety of his family and looked out on the wreck of a ruined world.

No Such Thing as Good Luck.—A parishioner asked a clergyman why the congregation had filled up and why the church was now so prosperous above what it had been before. "Well," said the clergyman, "I will tell you the secret. I met a tragedian some time ago, and I said to him, 'How is it you get along so well in your profession?' The tragedian replied, 'The secret is, I always do my best; when stormy days come and the theater is not more than half or a fourth occupied, I always do my best, and that has been the secret of my getting on.'" And the clergyman reciting it, said: "I have remembered that, and ever since then I have always done my best.'' And I say to you, in whatever occupation or profession God has put you, do your best; whether the world appreciates it or not, do your best—always do your best. Domitian, the Roman emperor, for one hour every day caught flies and killed them with his penknife; and there are people with imperial opportunity who set themselves to some insignificant business. Oh, for something grand to do, and then concenter all your energies of body and mind and soul upon that one thing, and nothing in earth or hell can stand before you. There is no such thing as good luck.

Lessons from the Turtle.—The plumage of the robin redbreast, the mottled sides of the Saranac trout, the upholstery of a spider's web, the waist of the wasp fashionably small without tight lacing, the lustrous eye of the gazelle, the ganglia of the starfish, have been discoursed upon; but it is left to us, fagged out from a long ramble, to sit down on a log and celebrate the admirable qualities of a turtle. We refer not to the curious architecture of its house —ribbed, plated, jointed, carapace and plastron, divinely fashioned—but its instincts, worthy almost of being called mental and moral qualities.

The tortoise is wiser than many people we wot of in the fact that he knows when to keep his head in his shell. No sooner did we just now appear on the edge of the wood than this animal of the order Testudinata modestly withdrew. He knew he was no match for us. But how many of the human race are in the habit of projecting their heads into things for which they have no fittedness. They thrust themselves into discussions where they are almost sure to get trod on. The first and last important lesson for such persons to learn is like this animal at our feet to shut up their shell, then they might become as wise as this turtle.

We admire also the turtle's capacity of being at home everywhere. He carries with him his parlor, nursery, kitchen, bedroom and bath-room. Would that we all had as equal facility of domestication! In such a beautiful world, and with so many comfortable surroundings, we ought to feel at home in any place we are called to be. While we cannot like the tortoise, carry our house on our back, we are better off for by the right culture of a contented spirit we may make the sky itself the mottled shell of our residence, and the horizon all around us shall be the place where the carapace shuts down on the plastron.

We admire still more the tortoise's determination to right itself. By way of experiment, turn it upside down, and then go off a piece to see it regain its position. Now there is nothing when put upon its back which has such a little prospect of getting to its feet again as this animal. One would think that a turtle once upside down would be upside down for ever.

But put it on its back and it keeps on scrabbling till it is right side up. We would like to pick up this animal from the dust and put it down on Broadway, if men passing by would learn from it never to stop exertion, even when overthrown. You can not by commercial disasters be more thoroughly flat on your back than five minutes ago was this poor thing. Do not lie still discouraged. Make an effort to get up. Throw your feet out first in one direction and then another. Scrabble.

We find from this day's roadside observation that the turtle uses its head before it does its feet; in other words it looks around before it moves. You never catch a turtle doing anything without previous careful inspection. We would all of us do better if we always looked before we leaped. It is easier to get into trouble than to get out. Better know where a road comes out before we start on it. Before starting a turtle always sticks its head out of its shell.

But tortoises die. They sometimes last two hundred years. They have a quiet life and no wear and tear upon their nervous system. Yet they after a while, notwithstanding all their slow travel reach the end of their journey. For the last time they draw their head inside their shell and shut out the world forever. Notwithstanding the useful thoughts they suggest while living, they are still more worth while when dead. We fashion their bodies into soup and their carapace into combs for the hair. Will we be useful when we are dead? Some men are tossed aside like a tortoise shell crushed by a cart wheel; but others by deeds done or words spoken, are useful long after they quit life, their examples are encouragement, their memory a banquet.

But we must be off this log, for the ants are crawling over us and the bull-frogs croak as though the night were coming on. The evening star hangs its lantern at the door of night to light the tired day to rest. The wild roses in the thicket are breathing vespers at an altar cushioned with moss while the fireflies are kindling their dim lamps in the cathedral of the woods. The evening dew on strings of fern is counting its beads in prayer.

PICTURES

The Power of Pictures.—In the reign of Charles the First it was ordered by Parliament that all pictures of Christ be burned. Painters were so badly treated and humiliated in the beginning of the eighteenth century that they were lowered clear down out of the sublimity of their art, and obliged to give accounts of what they did with their colors. The oldest picture in England, a portrait of Chaucer, though now of great value, was picked out of a lumber garret. Great were the trials of Quentin Matsys, who toiled on from blacksmith's anvil till, as a painter, he won wide recognition. The first missionaries to Mexico made the fatal mistake of destroying pictures, for the loss of which art and religion must ever lament. Oh, the power of pictures! I cannot deride, as some have done, Cardinal Mazarin, who, when told that he must die, took his last walk through the art-gallery of his palace, saying: "Must I quit all this? Look at that Titian! Look at that Correggio! Look at that 'Deluge' of Caracci! Farewell, dear pictures!"

Pictures, a Universal Language.—Pictures are not only a strong but a universal language. The human race is divided into almost as many languages as there are nations, but the pictures may speak of people of all tongues. Volapük, many have hoped, with little reason, would become a worldwide language; but the pictorial is always a worldwide language, and printers' types have no emphasis compared with it. We say that children are fond of pictures, but notice any man when he takes up a book, and you will see that the first thing that he looks at is the pictures. Have only those in your house that appeal to the better nature. One engraving has sometimes decided an eternal destiny. Your children will carry on to the grave the picture of their father's house and, passing that marble pillar, will take them through eternity.

PRAYER

Prayer a Power to Be Used Constantly.—I never

yet asked God to do anything but he did it, if it were for the best, and in all cases where my prayer has not been answered, I have found out afterward that it was best not to have been answered in my way. But none of us have tested the full power of prayer. It is a force very like some of the forces of nature, that were in existence but not employed. For ages electricity was thought good for nothing but to burn barns and kill people with one fell stroke. The lightning-rod on the top of houses was the spear with which the world charged on the thunderstorm, as much as to say: "If you dare to come this way, I will hurl you into the ground." But now electricity lightens homes and churches and cities and Christendom, and moves rail-cars; and he is a rash man who mentions anything as impossible to this natural energy. So the power of prayer was to the world rather a frightful power, if it was any power at all. But that has been changed and men begin to use it in some things. Mightier agent than any natural force yet developed will be this Gospel electricity, flashing heavenward for help, flashing earthward with divine response. God in business life. God in agricultural life. God in mechanical life. God in artistic life. God in every kind of life. Your religion for the most part is hung up so high you cannot reach it. It is hung up on the cloudy rafters of the sky where you expect to snatch it up as you finally go through for heavenly residence. Oh, have your religion within easy reach now! Religion is not for heaven, but for this world. Once in heaven, we will need no prayer, for we shall have everything we want.

Potency of Prayer.—When on the sea, Captain Haldane swore at the ship's crew with an oath that wished them all in perdition, and a Scotch sailor touched his cap and said, "Captain! God hears prayers, and we would be badly off if your wish were answered." Captain Haldane was convicted by the sailor's remark and converted, and became the means of salvation of his brother Robert, who had been an infidel; and then Robert became a minister of the Gospel and under his ministry the godless Felix Neff became the world-renowned missionary of the Cross and the worldly Merle d'Aubigne became the author of the History of the Reformation and will be the glory of the church for all ages. Perhaps you may do as much as the Scotch sailor, who just tipped his cap and used one broken sentence by which the earth and the heavens are still resounding with potent influences.

Agassiz' Prayer.—Agassiz standing amid his student explorers down in Brazil, coming across some great novelty in the rocks, taking off his hat said: "Gentlemen, let us pray; we must have divine illumination; we want wisdom from the Creator to study these rocks; he made them; let us pray."

John Q. Adams' Prayer.—It may be that in that hour of our departure we will be too feeble to say a long prayer. It may be in that hour we will not be able to say the "Lord's Prayer," for it has seven petitions. Perhaps we may be too feeble even to say the infant prayer our mothers taught us, which John Quincy Adams, seventy years of age, said every night when he put his head upon his pillow:

> Now I lay me down to sleep,
> I pray the Lord my soul to keep.

We may be too feeble to employ either of these familiar forms; but the prayer of Stephen is so short, is so concise, is so earnest, is so comprehensive, we surely will be able to say that: "Lord Jesus, receive my spirit."

Church Prayers.—Help ought to come through the prayers of many people. The door of the eternal store house is hung on one hinge—a golden hinge—the hinge of prayer, and when the whole audience lays hold of the door it must come open. There are people who have not been in church before for ten years; what will your prayer do for them by rolling over their soul holy memories? There are people who have risen in crises of awful temptation. They are on the verge of despair, or wild blundering, or theft, or suicide. What will your prayer do for them in the way of giving them strength to resist? There are many people spending their first Sabbath after some great bereavement. What will your prayers do for them? How will it help the tomb in that man's heart? Will you be chiefly anxious about the fit of the glove that you put to your forehead while in prayer? Will you be chiefly critical of the rhetoric of the pastor's petition? No, no, a thousand people should feel "that prayer is for me," at every step of the prayer chains ought to drop off, and temples of sin ought to crash into dust, and jubilees of deliverance ought to brandish their trumpets. In most of our churches we have three prayers: the opening prayer; what is called the "Long Prayer"; and the closing prayer. There are many people who spend their first prayer in arranging their apparel after entrance, and spend the second prayer, the "Long Prayer," in wishing it were through, and spending the last prayer in preparing to start for home. The most insignificant part of every religious service is the sermon. The most important parts are the Scripture lesson and the prayer. The sermon is only a man talking to a man. The Scripture lesson is God talking to a man. Prayer is man talking to God.

Oh, if we understood the grandeur and the pathos of this exercise of prayer, instead of being a dull exercise we would be imagining that the room was full of divine and angelic appearance.

Believing Prayer.—You are to seek the Lord with earnest and believing prayer. God is not an autocrat or a despot seated on a throne with his arms resting on brazen lions, and a sentinel pacing up and down at the foot of the throne. God is a father seated in a bower waiting for His children to come and climb on His knee, and get His kiss and His benediction. Prayer is the cup with which we go to the "fountain of living water" and dip up refreshment for our thirsty soul. Grace does not come to the heart as we set a cask at the corner of the house to catch the rain in the shower. It is a pulley fastened to the throne of God, which we pull, bringing the blessing. I do not care what posture you take in prayer nor how large an amount of voice you use; unless you pray right inwardly there will be no response. Prayers must be believing, earnest, loving. You are in your house some summer day and a shower comes up, and a bird, affrighted, darts into the window and wheels around the room. You seize it. You smooth its ruffled plumage. You feel its fluttering heart. You say, "Poor thing, poor thing." Now a prayer goes out of the storm of this world into the window of God's mercy and He catches it, and He feels the fluttering pulse, and He puts it in his own bosom of affection and safety. Prayer is a warm, ardent, pulsating exercise. It is the electric battery which touched, thrills to the throne of God! It is the diving-bell in which we go down into the depths of God's mercy and bring up "pearls of great price." Oh, how many wonderful things prayer has accomplished! In the days when the Scotch Covenanters were persecuted, and enemies were after them, one of the men among the Covenanters prayed: "O Lord, we be as dead men unless Thou shalt help us!" And instantly a Scotch mist enveloped and hid the persecuted from their persecutors—the promise literally fulfilled, "While they are yet speaking I will hear."

Faithful in Prayer.—I have a word of counsel, and that is, be faithful in prayer. You might as well, business man, start out in the morning without food and expect to be strong all that day—you might as well abstain from food all the week and expect to be strong physically as to be strong without prayer. The only way to get strength into the soul is by prayer, and the only difference between that Christian who is worth everything and that who is worth nothing is the fact that the latter does not pray and the other does.

You can graduate a man's progress in religion by the amount of prayer, not by the number of hours perhaps, but by the earnest supplication that he puts up to God. There is no exception to the rule. Show me a man who prays, and his strength and his power cannot be exaggerated. Just give to a man this power of prayer and you give him almost omnipotence.

Not one of us yet knows how to pray. All we have done has only been pottering and guessing and experimenting. A boy gets hold of his father's saw and hammer and tries to make something, but it is a poor affair. The father comes and takes the same saw and hammer and builds the house and ship. In the childhood of our Christian faith we make but poor work with these weapons of prayer. But when we come to the stature of men in Christ Jesus, then under these implements, the temple of God will rise and the world redemption be launched. God cares not for the length of our prayers, or the number of our prayers, or the beauty of our prayers, or the place of our prayers, but it is the faith in them that tells—believing that prayer soars higher than the lark ever sang, plunges deeper than diving-bell ever sank, darts quicker than lightning ever flashed. Though we have used only the back of this weapon instead of the edge, what marvels have been wrought!

There is no such detective as prayer, for no one can hide away from it. It puts its hand on a man ten thousand miles away. It lights on a ship mid-ocean. The little child cannot understand the law of electricity, or how the telegraph operator by touching an instrument here may dart a message under the sea to another continent; nor can we with our small intellects understand how the touch of a Christian's prayer shall instantly strike a soul on the other side of the earth. You take a ship and go to some other country, and get there at eleven o'clock in the morning. You cable New York and the message gets there at six o'clock in the same morning. In other words, it seems to arrive five hours before it started. Like that is prayer. God says, "Before they call I will hear." A boy running away from home may take the midnight train from the country village and reach the seaport in time to gain the ship that sails on the morrow, but a mother's prayer will be on the deck to meet him and in the hammock before he swings into it. There is a mightiness in prayer. The breath of Elijah's prayer blew all the clouds off the sky and it was dry weather. Prayer in Daniel's time walked the cave as a lion-tamer. It reached up and took the sun by its golden bit and stopped it. We have all yet to try the full power of prayer. If saved, we are all the captives of some earnest prayer. Would God that in desire for the rescue of souls, we might in prayer lay hold of the resources of the Lord Omnipotent.

PROCRASTINATION

Peril of Procrastination.—William III made proclamation, when there was a revolution in the north of Scotland, that all who came and took the oath of allegiance by the thirty-first of December should be pardoned. MacIan, a chieftain of a prominent clan, resolved to return with the rest of the rebels, but had some pride in being the very last one that should take the oath. He postponed starting for this purpose until two days before the expiration of the term. A snow-storm impeded his way, and before he got up to take the oath and receive pardon from the throne the time was up and past. While the others were set free, MacIan was miserably put to death. He started too late and arrived too late. In like manner some of you are in prospect of losing forever the amnesty of the Gospel. Many of you are going to be forever too late. Remember the irreparable mistake of MacIan!

This Is a Supernal Chance.—Alexander with his army used to surround a city, and then would lift a great light in token to the people that, if they surrendered before that light went out, all would be well; but if once the light went out, then the battering-rams would swing against the wall, and demolition would follow. All we need to do for our present and everlasting safety is to make surrender to Christ, the King and the Conqueror, surrender of our hearts, surrender of our lives, surrender of everything. And he keeps a great light burning, light of Gospel invitation, light kindled with the wood of the cross and flaming up against the dark night of our sin and sorrow. Surrender while that great light continues to burn, for after it goes out there will be no other opportunity of making peace with God through our Lord Jesus Christ. Talk of another chance! Why, this is a supernal chance.

Beached for Eternity.—I rode some thirteen miles to see the Alexander, a large steamship that was beached near Southampton, Long Island. It was a splendid vessel. As I walked up and down the decks and in the cabins, I said, "What a pity that this vessel should go to pieces, or be lying here idle!" The coast-wreckers had spent thirty thousand dollars trying to get her off, and they succeeded once; but she came back again to the old place. While I was walking on deck, every part of the vessel trembled with the beating of the surf on one side. Since then I heard that that vessel, which was worth hundreds of thousands of dollars, was sold for three thousand five hundred and knocked to pieces. They had given up the idea of getting her to sail again. How suggestive all that is to me! There are those here who are aground in religious things. Once you started for heaven, but you are now aground. Several times it was thought you had started again, heavenward, but you soon got back to the old place, and there is not much prospect you will ever reach the harbors of the blessed. God's wreckers, I fear, will pronounce you a hopeless case. Beached for eternity!

REMINISCENCE

Holiday Time.—There is something in the periodical holidays to bring up remembrances of the old folks. Sometimes in the winter holidays, when we are accustomed to gather our families together, old times have come back again, and our thoughts have been set to the tune of "Auld Lang Syne." The old folks seemed to be busy at such times in making us happy, and perhaps on less resource made their sons and daughters happier than you on larger resource are able to make your sons and daughters happy. The snow lay two feet above their graves, but they shook off the white blankets and mingled in the holiday festivities—the same wrinkles, the same stoop of shoulder under the weight of age, the same old style of dress or coat, the same smile, the same voice. I hope you remember them as they were before they went away.

While I Mused.—"While I was musing, the fire burned." Here is David, the Psalmist, with the forefinger of his right hand against his temple, and the door shut against the world, engaged in contemplation. And it would be well for us to take the same posture often, while we sit down in solitude to contemplate.

In a small island off the coast of Nova Scotia I once passed a Sabbath in delightful solitude, for I had resolved that I would have one day of entire quiet before I entered upon autumnal work. I thought to have spent the day in laying out plans for Christian work; but instead of that it became a day of tender reminiscence. I reviewed my pastorate; I shook hands with an old departed friend, whom I shall greet again when the curtains of life are lifted. The days of my boyhood came back and I was ten years of age, and I was eight, and I was five. There was but one house on the island, and yet from Sabbath daybreak, when the bird-chant woke me, until evening melted into the Bay of Fundy, from shore to shore where were ten thousand memories, and the groves were a-hum with voices that had long ago ceased.

Youth is apt too much to spend all its time in looking forward. Old age is apt too much to spend all its time in looking backward. People in mid-life and on the apex look both ways. It would be well for us, I think, however, to spend more time in reminiscence. By the constitution of our nature we spend most of the time looking forward. And the vast majority of people live not so much in the present as in the future. I find that you mean to make a reputation, you mean to establish yourself, and the advantages that you expect to achieve absorb a great deal of your time. But I see no harm in this, if it does not make you discontented with the present, or disqualify you for existing duties. It is a useful thing sometimes to look back and to see the dangers we have escaped, and to see the sorrows we have suffered, and the trials and wanderings of earthly pilgrimage and to sum up our enjoyments.

There is a chapel in Florence with fresco by Giotto. It was covered up with two inches of stucco until after our American and European artists went there and after long toil removed the covering and retraced the fresco. I am aware that the memory of the past with many of you is all covered up with obliterations, but take away the covering, that the old picture may shine out again.

THE SEASONS

Spring—Autumn—Winter.—The *spring* is suggestive of God and heaven and the resurrection day. That eye must be blind that does not see God's footstep in the new grass, and hear his voice in the call of the swallow at the eaves. In the white blossoms of the orchards we find suggestion of those whose robes have been made white in the blood of the Lamb. A May morning is a door opening into heaven.

So *autumn* mothers a great many moral and religious suggestions. The season of corn husking, the gorgeous woods that become the catafalque of the dead year remind the dullest of his own fading and departure.

Winter is just as important as the spring. Let one winter pass without frost to kill vegetation and ice to bind the rivers and snow to enrich our field, and then you will have to enlarge your hospitals and your cemeteries. Storms to purify the air. Thermometer at ten degrees above zero to tone up the system. December and January just as important as May and June. We need the storms of life as much as we do the sunshine. I am glad to believe that the monsoons and typhoons, and mistrals, and siroccos of the land and sea are not unchained maniacs let loose upon the earth, but under divine supervision! It was out of Dante's suffering came the sublime "Divina Commedia," and out of John Milton's blindness came "Paradise Lost," and out of your bereavement, your persecution, your poverties, your misfortunes may yet come an eternal heaven.

SERVICE

Ordinary Duty in Ordinary Places.—The Earl of Kintore said to me on an English railway: "Mr. Talmage, when you get back to America I want you to preach a sermon on the discharge of ordinary duty in ordinary places, and then send me a copy of it." Afterward, an English clergyman coming to this land brought from the Earl of Kintore the same message. Alas! before I got ready to do what he asked me to do, the good Earl of Kintore had departed this life. But that man, surrounded by all palatial surroundings and in a distinguished sphere felt sympathetic with those who had ordinary duties to perform in ordinary places and in ordinary ways. A great many people are discouraged when they hear the story of Moses and of Joshua and of David and of Luther and of John Knox and of Deborah and of Florence Nightingale. They say, "Oh, that was all good and right for them, but I shall never be called to command the sun and the moon to stand still. I shall never be called to slay a giant. I shall never preach on Mars Hill. I shall never defy the Diet of Worms. I shall never be able to make a queen tremble for her crimes. I shall never preside over a hospital." There are women who say: "If I had as brilliant a sphere as those people had, I should be as brave and as grand; but my business is to get the children off to school, and to hunt up things when they are lost, and to see that dinner is ready, and to keep account of the household expenses, and to keep the children from being strangulated by the whooping cough, and to go through all the annoyances and vexations of housekeeping. Oh, my sphere is so infinitesimal and so insignificant, I am clear discouraged." Woman, God places you on garrison duty and your reward will be just as great as that of Florence Nightingale, who moving so often night by night with a light in her hand through the hospitals, was called by the wounded the "Lady of the Lamp." Rewards are not given according to the amount of noise you make in the world, nor even according to the amount you do, but according to whether you work to your full capacity, according to whether you do your full duty in the sphere where God has placed you.

Two Kinds of Service.—Charles Reade, the great writer, lost the joint of his forefinger by feeding a

bear. Look out that your whole hand gets not into
the maw of the old Cerberus of perdition. Sir
Thomas Trotbridge, at the battle of Inkermann, lost
his foot, and when the soldiers would carry him
away he said, "No, I do not move until the battle
is won." So, if the foot be lamed or lost, let it be
in the service of our God, our home, or our
country.

Inconspicuous Service.—The impression is abroad
that the Christian rewards are for those who do
conspicuous service in distinguished places—great
martyrs, great patriots, great preachers, great
philanthropists. But my text sets forth the idea
that there is just as much reward for a man who
stays at home and minds his own business, and who,
crippled and unable to go forth and lead in great
movements and in high places of the earth, does his
whole duty just where he is. Garrison duty is as
important and as remunerative as service at the
front. "As his part is that goeth down to the battle, so shall his part be that tarrieth by the stuff."

A Quick Service.—Our business is to serve our
own generation, the people now living, those whose
lungs now breathe and whose hearts now beat. And
mark you, it is not a silent procession, but moving.
It is a "forced march" at twenty-four miles a day,
each hour being a mile. Going with that celerity it
has got to be a quick service on our part, or no service at all. We not only cannot teach the one hundred and eighty generations past, and will not see
the one hundred generations to come, but this generation now on the stage will soon be off, and we
ourselves will be off with them. The fact is that
you and I have to start very soon for our work, or
it will be ironical and sarcastic for any one after
our exit to say of us as it was said of David,

"After he had served his own generation by the will of God, he fell on sleep."

The Most Triumphant Thing.—Sometimes in life it is necessary to make a retort; sometimes in life it is necessary to resist; but there are crises when the most triumphant thing to do is to keep silence. The philosopher, confident in his newly discovered principle, waiting for the coming of more intelligent generations, willing that men should laugh at the lightning-rod, the cotton-gin, and steamboat, waiting for long years through the scoffing of philosophical schools, in grand and magnificent silence.

Galileo, condemned by mathematicians and monks and cardinals, caricatured everywhere, yet waiting and watching with his telescope to see the coming up of stellar reënforcements, when the stars in their courses would fight for the Copernican system; then sitting down in complete blindness and deafness to wait for the coming on of the generations who would build his monument and bow at his grave. The reformer execrated by his contemporaries, fastened in a pillory, the slow fires of public contempt burning under him, ground under the cylinders of the printing press, yet calmly waiting for the day when purity of soul and heroism of character will get the sanction of earth and the plaudits of heaven.

Affliction endured without complaint—the heft of the chain—the darkness of the night—waiting until a Divine hand shall be put forth to soothe the pang, and hush the storm, and release the captive.

Make no Answer.—If you are assailed by jealousy, make no answer. Take it as a compliment, for people are never jealous of a failure. Until your work is done you are invulnerable. Remember how your Lord behaved under exasperations. Did they not

try to catch Him in His word? Did they not call
Him the victim of intoxicants? Did they not misinterpret Him from the winter of the year 1 to the
spring 33—that is from His first infantile cry to the
last groan of His assassination? Yet He answered
not a word. But so far from demolishing either
His mission or His good name, after nineteen centuries He outranks everything under the skies, and
is second to none above them, and the archangel
makes salaam at his footstool. Christ's bloody an-
tagonists thought that they had finished Him when
they wrote over the cross His accusation in three
languages—Hebrew, Greek, and Latin—not realiz-
ing that they were by the act introducing Him to
all nations, since Hebrew is the holiest language,
and Greek is the wisest of tongues, and Latin the
widest spoken.

Silence in Heaven.—The busiest place in the universe is heaven. It is the center from which all
good results arrive. The Bible represents it as active with wheels, and wings and orchestras, and
processions mounted or charioted. But my text describes a space when the wheels ceased to roll and
the trumpets to sound and the voices to chant. The
riders on the white horses reined in their chargers.
The doxologies were hushed and the processions
halted. The hand of arrest was upon all the splendors. "Stop, heaven!" cried an omnipotent voice,
and it stopped. For thirty minutes everything celestial stood still. "There was silence in heaven for
the space of half an hour." From all we can learn
it is the only time heaven ever stopped.

The Loudest Thing on Earth is Silence.—Oh, the
power of patient silence! Æschylus, the immortal
poet, was condemned to death for writing something
that offended the people. All the pleas in his behalf

were of no avail, until his brother uncovered the arm of the prisoner and showed that his hand had been shot off at Salamis. That silent plea liberated him. The loudest thing on earth is silence if it be of the right kind and at the right time.

SNOW

Accumulated Power.—Grossly maligned is the season of winter. The spring and summer and autumn have had many admirers; but winter hoary-headed and white-bearded hath more enemies than friends. Yet without winter the human race would be inane and effortless. You might speak of the winter as the mother of tempests; but I take it as the father of a whole family of physical, mental and spiritual energies. Most of the people are strong in proportion to the number of snowbanks they had to climb over, or push through in childhood, while their fathers drove the sled loaded with logs through the crunching drifts high as the fences. At the season of the year when we are familiar with the snow—those frozen vapors, those fallen blossoms of the sky, those white angels of the atmosphere, those poems of the storm, I turn to my Bible and though most of it was written in a clime where snow seldom fell—I find many references to these beautiful congelations. Though the writers may seldom or never have felt the cold touch of the snowflake on their cheek, they had in sight two mountains, the tops of which were suggestive. Other kings sometimes take off their crowns, but Lebanon and Mount Hermon all the year round and through the ages never lift the coronets of crystals from their foreheads. The snow is not fully recognized in the Bible until God interrogates Job, the scientist, concerning its wonders, saying: "Hast thou entered into the treasures of the snow?" Oh, it is a wondrous meteor! When I see the Maker of the Universe giving himself to the architecture of a snowflake and making its shafts, its domes, its curves, its walls, its irradiations so perfect I conclude he will look after our insignificant affairs, and if we are of more value than a sparrow, most certainly we are of infinitely greater value than an inanimate snowflake. So the Bible would impress us with God in the littles. It does not say, "Consider the clouds," but it says, "Consider the lilies." Nothing is big to God and nothing is small. When you tell me that he is God of Mercury and the God of Saturn, you tell me something so vast that I cannot comprehend it. But if you tell me he is God of the snowflake you tell me something I can hold and measure and realize. Thus the smallest snowflake contains a jewel-case of comfort.

The snow is the treasure of accumulated power. During a snowstorm let an apothecary accustomed to weigh most delicate quantities, hold his weighing scales out of the window and let one flake fall on the surface of the scales and it will not even make it tremble. When you want to express extreme triviality of weight you say, "Light as a feather," but a snowflake is much lighter. And yet the accumulation of these flakes once broke down in sight of my house, six telegraph poles, it made helpless police and fire departments, and halted rail trains with two thundering locomotives. We have learned so much of the power of electricity that we have become careful how we touch the electric wire, and in many cases a touch means death. But the snow puts its hand on many of these wires and tears them down as though they were cobwebs. The snow puts its finger on the lips of our cities that are talking to each other and they relapse into silence, uttering not a word. The snow is mightier than the lightning!

In March, 1888, the snow stopped America. It said to New York, "Stay at home," to Philadelphia,

"Stay at home," to Washington, "Stay at home," to Richmond, "Stay at home." It put into a white sepulcher most of this nation. Commerce whose wheels never stopped before, stopped then. What was the matter? Power of accumulated snowflakes. Avalanches made up of single snowflakes. Snowslides of our own Northwest, many perishing by them every spring; snowslides on Alaskan glaciers, forever entombing the unfortunate gold-seekers; the melting snows flooding our great rivers, till they overleap their banks and carry destruction and death through entire counties along the Mississippi, the Missouri, the Ohio, and the Kansas. What a suggestion of accumulative power, and what a rebuke to all of us who get discouraged because we cannot do much and therefore do nothing, who will not be a snowflake because they cannot be an avalanche.

SONGS

National Songs.—I never shall forget hearing a Frenchman sing the "Marseillaise" on the Champs Elysees, Paris, just before the battle of Sedan in 1870. I never saw such enthusiasm before or since. As he sang that national air, how the Frenchmen shouted! Have you ever, in an English assemblage, heard the band play "God Save the Queen?" If you have, you know something about the enthusiasm of a national air. Now, I tell you that these songs we sing, Sabbath by Sabbath, are the national airs of Jesus Christ and of the kingdom of heaven, and if you do not learn to sing them here, how do you ever expect to sing the song of Moses and the Lamb?

Songs of Victory.—When Cromwell's army went into battle, he stood at the head of them one day, and gave out the long-meter doxology to the tune of

"Old Hundred," and that great host, company by company, regiment by regiment, brigade by brigade, joined in the doxology. And while they sang they marched, and while they marched they fought, and while they fought they got the victory. O, men and women of Jesus Christ, let us go into all our conflicts singing the praises of God, and then, instead of falling back, as we often do, from defeat to defeat, we will be marching on from victory to victory.

Songs of Earth.—The earth was fitted up for the human race, in congratulation the morning stars sang a song. The Israelitish army safe on the bank of the Red Sea and the Egyptians clear under the returned water, Moses sang a song. One of the most important parts of the great old Book is Solomon's song. At the birth of our Lord, the Virgin Mary and old Simeon and angelic prima donnas in hovering clouds sang a song. What enrichment has been given to the world's literature and enjoyment by the ballads, the canticles, the discants, the ditties, the roundelays, the epics, the lyrics, the dithyrambs.

"I Was the Song of the Drunkards."—Who said that? Was it David or was it Christ? It was both. These Messianic Psalms are like a telescope. Pull the instrument to a certain range and it shows you an object nearby. Pull it to another range, and it will show you objects far away. David and Christ were both, each in his own time, the song of the drunkards. Holiness of doctrine and life always did excite wicked merriment. Although David had fully reformed and written a psalmody in which all subsequent ages have sobbed out their penitence, his enemies preferred to fetch up his old career, and put into metric measures sins long before forgiven. Christ, who committed no sin, was still more the subject of unholy song, because the better one is, the more iniquity hates him. Notice that the second noun of my text is in the plural. Not "Drunkard," but "Drunkards." It would be dull work to sing that song solitary and alone. It is generally a chorus. They are in groups. On that downward way there must be companionship. Here and there is a man so mean as always to drink alone; but generous men, big-hearted men, drinking at bar or in restaurant or in club-house, feel mortified to take the average unaccompanied. There must be some one with whom to click the rim of the glasses, some one's health to propose, some sentiment to toast. There must be two, and still better if four, and still better if six, to give zest to the Song of the Drunkards.

Suggestion in Song.—There is a suggestion in song. You hear a nursery refrain, and right away you think of your childhood home, and brothers and sisters with whom you played, and mother long since gone to rest. You hear a national air, and you think of the encampment of 1863, and the still night on the river bank, and the camp-fires that shook their reflections up and down the faces of the regiment. You hear an old church tune, and you are reminded of the revival scenes amid which you were brought to God. Nothing so brings up associations as a song sung or played upon an instrument.

Cradle Songs.—Standing at Bethlehem, I thought that the most honored thing in all the earth is the cradle. To what else did loosened star ever point? To what else did heaven lower balconies of light filled with chanting immortals? That cradle song in Bethlehem should have its echo in our cradle songs. The songs our mothers sang to us when they put us to sleep are singing yet. We may have forgotten the words, but they went to the fiber of our soul and will forever be a part of it. It is not so much what you formally teach your children as what you sing to them. A hymn has wings and can fly everywhither. One hundred and fifty years after you are dead grandchildren will be singing the song which you now sing to your little ones gathered at your knee. There is a place in Switzerland where if you distinctly utter your voice there comes back ten or fifteen distinct echoes. Every Christian song sung by a mother in the ear of her child shall have 10,000 echoes coming back from the gates of heaven.

Songs of Heaven.—There is a legend that when people entered the Temple of Diana in olden times, sometimes their eyesight was extinguished by the brilliancy of the room, the gold and the glitter of the precious stones, and therefore the janitor when he introduced strangers into that room always said to them: "Take heed to your eyes." The stranger entered that room with shaded vision. But, O my friends, when the song of the redeemed rises about the throne, many-voiced and multitudinous, you take heed of your ears—the song so loud and so stupendous. They sing a rock song, saying: "Who is he that sheltered us in the wilderness, and was the shadow of a great rock in a weary land?" and the chorus comes in: "Christ, the shadow of a great rock in a weary land." They sing a star song, saying: "Who is he that guided us through the night and when all other lights went out shone on us, the morning star for the world's darkness," and the chorus will come in, "Christ, the morning star for the world's darkness." They sing a flower song, saying: "Who is he that brightened the way for us and breathed perfume into our soul, and bloomed on through frost and tempest?" and the response of the chorus will come in, "Christ, the Lily of the Valley, blooming through frost and tempest." Yea, they sing a water song, saying: "Who is he that gleamed upon us through the top of the rock and brightened all the ravines of earthly trouble, and was a fountain in the midst of the wilderness?" and the chorus will come in, "Christ, the fountain in the midst of the wilderness." Are we to-day rehearsing for it?

Nations Fall Like Stars.—God sets nations to revolve as stars, but they may fall. Tyre—the atmosphere of the desert fragrant with spices, coming in caravans to her fairs; all seas cleft into foam by the keels of her laden merchantmen; her markets rich with horses and camels from Togarmah; her bazaars filled with upholstery from Dedan, with emeralds and coral and agate from Seria, with wines from Helbon, with embroidered work from Ashur and Chilmad. Where now the gleam of her towers, where the roar of her chariots, where the masts of her ships? Let the fishermen who dry their nets where she once stood; let the sea that rushes upon the barrenness where once she challenged the admiration of all nations; let the barbarians who set their rude tents where once her palaces glittered, answer the question. She was a star; but by her own sin has fallen. Hundred-gated Thebes—for all time to be the study of antiquarian and hieroglyphist; her stupendous ruins spread over twenty-seven miles; her sculptures presenting in figures of warrior and chariot the victories with which the now-forgotten kings of Egypt shook the nations; her obelisks and columns; Karnak and Luxor, the stupendous temples of her pride. Thebes built not one temple to God. Thebes hated righteousness and loved sin. Thebes was a star, but she has fallen. Babylon—with her two hundred and fifty towers and her brazen gates and her embattled walls, the splendor of the earth gathered within her palaces, her hanging gardens built by Nebuchadnezzar to please his bride Amytis, who had been brought up in a country round Babylon; these hanging gardens built terrace above terrace, till the height of four hundred feet, there were woods waving and fountains playing—the verdure, the foliage, the glory, looking as if a mountain were on wing. On the tip-top a king walking with his queen, among statues snowy white, looking up at the birds brought from distant lands, and drinking out of tankards of solid gold, or looking off over rivers and lakes upon nations subdued and tributary, crying: "Is not this great Babylon which I have built?" Babylon was proud, Babylon was impure, Babylon was a star, but by sin she has fallen.

The Star of Wormwood.—Rev. 8: 10,11: "There fell a great star from heaven burning as it were a lamp, and it fell upon the third part of the rivers, and upon the fountains of waters; and the name of the star is called Wormwood." Are any of you the star Wormwood? Do you scold and growl from the thrones paternal or maternal? Are you always crying "Hush!" to the merry voices and swift feet and the laughter, which occasionally trickles through at wrong times, and is suppressed by them until they can hold it no longer, and all the barriers burst into unlimited guffaw and cachinnation, as in time of freshet the water has trickled through a slight opening in the mill-dam, but afterward makes wider and wider the breach until it carries all before it with irresistible flood? Do not be too much offended at the noise your children now make. It will be still enough when one of them is dead. Then you would give your right hand to hear one shout from their silent voices, or one step from the still foot. You will not any of you have to wait very long before your house is stiller than you want it. What is your influence upon the neighborhood, the town, or the city of your residence? I will suppose that you are a star of wit. What kind of rays do you shoot forth? Do you use that splendid faculty to irradiate the world or to rankle it? You are a star of worldly prosperity. Then you have large opportunity. You can bless the world. Suppose you are selfish and overbearing and arrogant. Then you are the star Wormwood, and you have embittered one-third, if not three-thirds, of the waters that roll past your employees and operatives and dependents and associates. What kind of a star are you?

Morning and Evening Stars.—Some of you, I know, are morning stars, and you are making the dawning life of your children bright with gracious influences, and you are beaming upon all the opening enterprises of philanthropic and Christian endeavor, and you are heralds of that day of Gospelization which will yet flood all the mountains and valleys of our sin-cursed earth. Hail, morning star! Keep on shining with encouragement and Christian hope! Some of you are evening stars, and you are cheering the last days of old people; and though a cloud sometimes comes over you through the querulousness or unreasonableness of your father and mother, it is only for a moment, and the star soon comes out clear again and is seen from all the balconies of the neighborhood. The old people will forgive your occasional shortcomings, for they themselves several times lost their patience with you when you were young. Hail, evening star!

Hang on the darkening sky your diamond coronet.

"Shall Shine as the Stars."—The Bible promises to all the faithful, eternal luster, they "shall shine as the stars forever."

Look up at the night, see each world show its distinct glory. It is not like the conflagration in which you cannot tell where one flame stops and another begins. Neptune, Herschel and Mercury are as distinct as if each one of them were the only star; so our individualism will not be lost in heaven. A great multitude—yet each one as observable, as distinctly recognized, as greatly celebrated, as if in all the space, from gate to gate and from hill to hill he were the only inhabitant; no mixing up, no mob, no indiscriminate rush, each Christian standing illustrious—all the story of earthly achievement adhering to each one. They shall shine with distinct light forever and ever. The same stars that look down upon us looked down upon the Chaldean shepherds. Adam saw coming through the dusk of the evening the same worlds that greet us now. The star at which the mariner looks to-night was the light by which the ships of Tarshish were guided across the Mediterranean, and the Venetian flotilla found its way into Lepanto. Their armor is as bright to-night as when in ancient battle the stars in their courses fought against Sisera.

To the ancients the stars were the symbols of eternity. But the Bible says they shall fall like autumn leaves. Star after star shall be carried out to burial amid funeral torches of burning worlds. But the Christian workers shall never leave their thrones—they shall reign forever and ever.

Ministers of Religion.—Turn now in your Bible to the seven stars. We are distinctly told that they are the ministers of religion. Some are large stars, some of them small stars, some of them sweep a wide circuit and some of them a small circuit, but so far as they are genuine, they get their light from the great central Sun, around whom they make revolution. Let each one keep in his own sphere. The solar system would be soon wrecked if the stars, instead of keeping their own orbits, should go to hunting down other stars. Ministers of religion should never clash. But in all the centuries of the Christian church, some of these stars have been hunting an Edward Irving or a Horace Bushnell or an Albert Barnes; and the stars that were in pursuit of the other stars lost their own orbit, and some of them could never again find it. Alas for the heresy hunters! The best way to destroy error is to preach the truth. The best way to scatter darkness is to strike a light. There is in immensity room enough for all the ministers. The ministers who give up righteousness and the truth will get punishment enough anyhow, for they are "the wandering stars for whom is reserved the blackness of darkness forever."

TIME

Three Inscriptions.—There are three inscriptions over the three doors of the Cathedral of Milan. Over one door, amid a wreath of sculptured roses, I read: "All that which pleases us is but for a moment." Over another door around a sculptured cross, I read: "All that which troubles us is but for a moment." But over the central door, I read: "That only is important which is eternal." Oh, Eternity! Eternity! Eternity!

Eternity!—Eternity is too big a subject for us to understand. Some one has said it is a great clock, that says "Tick" in one century, and "Tack" in another. But we can better understand Old Time, who has many children, and they are the centuries, and many grandchildren, and they are the years.

Half-hours.—That half-hour mentioned in my text is more widely known than any other period in the calendar of heaven. None of the whole hours of heaven are measured off, none of the years, none of the centuries. Of the millions of ages past, and the millions of ages to come, not one is especially measured off in the Bible. But the half-hour of my text is made immortal. The only part of eternity that was ever measured by earthly timepiece was measured by the minute hand of my text. Oh, the half-hours! They decide everything. I am not asking what you will do with the years or months or days of your life, but what of the half-hours. Tell me the history of your half-hours, and I will tell you the story of your whole life on earth and the story of your whole life in eternity. The right or wrong things you can say in thirty minutes are glorious or baleful, inspiring or desperate. Look out for the fragments of time. They are pieces of eternity. It was the half-hours between the duties as schoolmaster that made Salmon P. Chase chief-justice, the half-hours between shoe-lasts that made Henry Wilson vice-president of the United States, the half-hours between canal-boats that made James A. Garfield president. The half-hour a day for good books or bad books; the half-hour a day for prayer or indolence; the half-hour a day for helping others or blasting others; the half-hour before you go to business; that makes the difference between the scholar and the ignoramus, between the Christian and the infidel, between the saint and the demon, between triumph and catastrophe, between heaven and hell.

The most tremendous things of your life and mine were certain half-hours.

Measuring Our Days and Nights.—I have heard that Alfred, the king, before the invention of time-pieces, used to measure the day by three wax candles. Each wax candle would burn eight hours, so that when one candle was consumed eight hours were gone; two candles, sixteen hours were gone; and when the third wax candle had been consumed, then the twenty-four hours—the whole day—was gone. Oh, I wish instead of measuring our days and nights and years on earth by a timepiece we would measure time by mercies and opportunities, which are burning down and out, never to be relighted, lest we wake up with the discomfiture of the foolish virgins, and cry, "Our lamps are gone out!"

Stray Moments.—How many there are in this gay world who say they are so busy they have no time for mental, or spiritual improvement; the great duties of life cross the field like strong reapers and carry off all the hours, and there is only here and there a fragment left that is worth gleaning. Ah, my friends, you could go into the busiest day and busiest week of your life and find golden opportunities, which gathered, might at least make a whole sheaf for the Lord's garner. It is the stray opportunities, and the stray privileges, which taken up and bound together and beaten out will at last fill you with abounding joy.

There are a few moments worth the gleaning. Now to the field! May each one have a measure full and running over! If there is in your household an aged one or a sick relative that is not strong enough to come forth and toil in this field, then let Ruth take home to Naomi this sheaf of gleaning; "He that goeth forth and weepeth, bearing precious seed; shall doubtless come again rejoicing, bringing his sheaves with him.''

Short but Vast Opportunity.—The year is a great wheel and there is a band on that wheel that keeps it revolving, and as that wheel turns it turns three hundred and sixty-five wheels, which are the days, and then each of these wheels turns twenty-four smaller wheels which are the hours, and these twenty-four smaller wheels turn sixty smaller wheels, which are the minutes, and these sixty smaller wheels turn sixty smaller wheels, which are the seconds, and they keep rolling, rolling, rolling, mounting, mounting, mounting, swiftening, swiftening, swiftening. O God! If our generation is going like that and we are going with them, waken us to the short but vast opportunity.

Value of Time.—Elihu Burritt learned many things while toiling in a blacksmith's shop. Abercrombie, the world-renowned philosopher, was a philosopher in Scotland, and he got his philosophy, or the chief part of it, while, as a physician he was waiting for the door of the sick-room to open.

TROUBLE

Keats' Trouble.—Keats wrote his famous poem, and hard criticism of the poem killed him—literally killed him. Tasso wrote his poem, entitled ''Jerusalem Delivered,'' and it had such a cold reception it turned him into a raving maniac. Stillingfleet was slain by his literary enemies. The frown of Henry VIII slew Cardinal Wolsey. The Duke of Wellington refused to have ,the fence around his house, which had been destroyed by an excited mob, repaired, because he wanted the fence to remain as it was, a reminder of the mutability and uncertainty of popular favor.

And you will have trial of some sort. You have had it already. Why need I prophesy?

French Proverb.—A French proverb said that trouble comes in on horseback and goes away on foot. So trouble dashed in on you suddenly, but oh, how long it was in getting away! Came on horseback, goes away on foot.

Trials for Some Particular Purpose.—My friends, God intended these troubles and trials for some particular purpose. They do not come at random. In the Tower of London the swords and the guns of other ages are burnished and arranged into huge passion-flowers, and huge sunflowers, and bridal cakes, and you wonder how anything so hard as steel could be put into such floral shapes. I have to tell you that the hardest, sharpest, most cutting, most piercing sorrows of this life may be made to bloom and put on bridal festivity.

Lexicography of Trouble.—Our lexicographers, aware of the immense necessity of having plenty of words to express the different shades of trouble have strewn over their pages such words as "annoyance," "misery," "distress," "grief," "bitterness," "torture," "affliction," "anguish," "tribulation," "wretchedness," "war." But I have a glad sound for every hospital, for every sick room, for every life-long invalid, for every broken heart. "There shall be no more pain." Thank God! Thank God! No malarias. No weary arm. No painful respiration. No hectic flush. No one can drink of that healthy fountain and keep faint-hearted or faint-headed. He whose foot touches that pavement becometh an athlete. The first kiss of that summer air will take the wrinkles from the old man's cheek. Amid the multitude of songsters, not one diseased throat. The first flash of the throne will scatter the darkness of those who were born blind. See, the lame man leaps as a hart, and the dumb sing.

Tonics Nearly Always Bitter.—You want at least two misfortunes, hard as flint, to strike fire. Heavy and long-continued snows in the winter are signs of good crops next summer. So, many have yielded wonderful harvests of benevolence and energy because they were for a long while snowed under. We must have a good many hard falls before we learn to walk straight. Tonics are nearly always bitter.

This World an Insufficient Portion.—Nothing like trouble to show us that this world is an insufficient portion. Hogarth was about done with life, and he wanted to paint the end of all things. He put on canvas a shattered bottle; a cracked bell; an unstrung harp; a signboard of a tavern called "The World's End" falling down; a shipwreck; the horses of Phoebus lying dead in the clouds; the moon in her last quarter, and the world on fire. "One thing more," said Hogarth, "and my picture is done." Then he added the broken palette of a painter. Then he died.

Trouble Develops Character.—Especial trials fit for special work. Just watch and you will see that trouble is preparative and educational. That is the grindstone on which battle-axes are sharpened. I have always noticed in my own case that when the Lord had some especial work for me to do it was preceded by especial attack on me. This is so proverbial in my own house that if for something I say or do I get poured upon me a volley of censure and anathema, my wife always asks, "I wonder what new opportunity of usefulness is about to open? Something good and grand is surely coming.'' That is a very unfortunate man who has no trouble. Misfortune and trials are great educators. Sorrow—I see its touch in the grandest painting; I hear its tremor in the sweetest music; I feel its power in the mightiest argument.

Grecian mythology said that the fountain of Hippocrene was struck out by the foot of the winged horse Pegasus. I have often noticed in life that the brightest and most beautiful fountains of Christian comfort and spiritual life have been struck out by the iron hoof of disaster and calamity. I see Daniel's courage best by the flash of Nebuchadnezzar's furnace. I see Paul's prowess best when I find him on the floundering ship under the glare of the lightning in the breakers of Melita. God crowns his children amid the howling of wild beasts, and the chopping of blood-splashed guillotine, and the cracking of martyrdom. It took the stormy sea, and the December blast and the desolate New England coast, and the war-whoop of savages to show forth the prowess of the Pilgrim Fathers.

How to Meet Trouble.—No cavern is so deeply cleft in the mountains as to allow you shelter from trouble. The foot of the fleetest courser is not swift enough to bear you beyond pursuit. The arrows brought to the string fly with unerring dart, and often you have fallen pierced and stunned.

One man flies to prayer, another man stimulates himself with ardent spirits, another man dives deeper into secularities. It is not wonderful when a man sees his eternity poised on an uncertainty that he is determined to do something violent and immediate.

Every one comes during the course of life to be pummeled. Some slander comes at you horned and tusked and heeled, to trample and gore you, and you think you are peculiar in that respect. No. If you are able to say, "I haven't an enemy in all the world," it is proof positive you have not done your duty; for when a man does his duty he challenges all earth and hell, and that challenge will bring against him opposition, scorn, and persecution. It is so in all circles of life.

But if you try to carry your sins and your burdens yourself, I tell you, life will be a failure, your death will be disaster, and eternity a calamity; but if you will go to Christ with all your sins, and all your sorrows to-day, your foot will strike the upward path, and the shining messengers who tell above what is done here will make the arches of God resound with the tidings that you have gone to tell Jesus.

At Eventide.—"At evening time it shall be light." This prophecy will be fulfilled in the evening of Christian sorrow. For a long time it is broad daylight. The sun rises high. Innumerable activities go ahead, with a thousand feet and work with a thousand arms, and the pickax struck a mine, and the battery made a discovery, and the investment yielded its twenty per cent, and the book came to its twentieth edition, and the farm quadrupled in value, and sudden fortune hoisted to high position, and children were praised, and friends without number swarmed into the family hive, and prosperity sang in the music and stepped in the dance and glowed in the wine and ate at the banquet, and all the gods of music and ease and gratification gathered around this Jupiter, holding in his hands so many thunderbolts of power. But every sun must set, and the brightest day must have its twilight. Suddenly the sky was overcast. The fountain dried up. The song hushed. The wolf broke into the family fold and carried off the best lamb. A deep howl of woe came crashing down through the joyous symphonies. At one rough twang of the hand of disaster the harp-strings all broke. Did the night of their disaster come upon them moonless, starless, dark, and howling; smothering and choking their life out? No, no! At eventime it was light. The swift promises overtook them.

God's Pruning.—A grapevine says, in the early spring, "How glad I am to get through the winter! I shall have no more trouble now! Summer weather will come, and the garden will be very beautiful!" But the gardener comes, and cuts the vine here and there with his knife. The twigs begin to fall, and the grapevine calls out, "Murder! What are you cutting me for?" "Ah," says the gardener, "I don't mean to kill you. If I did not do this you would be the laughing-stock of all the other vines before the season is over." Months go on, and one day the gardener comes under the trellis, where great clusters of grapes hang, and the grapevine says, "Thank you, sir; you could not have done any-thing so kind as to have cut me with that knife." "Whom the Lord loveth he chasteneth." "Every branch that beareth fruit he purgeth that it may bring forth more fruit." No pruning, no grapes; no grinding-mill, no flour; no battle, no victory; no cross, no crown.

UPPER FORCES

Faith in the Upper Armies.—If the low levels of life are filled with armed threats and dangers, I have to tell you that the mountains of our hope, and courage and faith are full of the horses and chariots of divine rescue, "And behold the moun-tain was full of horses and chariots of fire round about Elisha."

Notice that the divine equipage is always represented as a chariot of fire. Ezekiel and Isaiah and John, when they come to describe the divine equipage, always represent it as a wheeled, harnessed, and upholstered conflagration. It is not a chariot like kings and conquerors of earth mount, but an organized and a compressed fire. That means purity, justice, chastisement, deliverance through burning escapes. Chariot of rescue? Yes, but chariot of fire.

How do I know that this divine equipage is on the side of our institutions? I know it by the history of the last hundred years. The American Revolution started by the pen of John Hancock in Independence Hall in 1776. The colonies without ships, without ammunition, without guns, without trained warriors, without money, without prestige. On the other side the mightiest nation in the world, the largest armies, and the grandest navies and the most distinguished commanders, and resources inexhaustible and nearly all nations ready to back them up in the fight. Nothing, as against immensity. The cause of the American colonies, which started at zero, dropped still lower, through the quarreling of the generals, and through jealousies amid small successes, and through the winters which surpassed all their predecessors in depth of snow and horrors of congealment. Elisha surrounded by the whole Syrian army did not seem to be worse off than did the thirteen colonies encompassed and overshadowed by foreign assault. What decided the contest in our favor? The upper forces, the upper armies. The Green and White Mountains of New England, the Highlands along the Hudson, the mountains of Virginia, all the Appalachian ranges were full of reenforcements which the young man Washington saw in faith and his men endured the frozen feet, and the gangrened wounds and the exhausting hunger, and the long march, because "The Lord opened the eyes of the young man; and he saw, and behold, the mountains were full of horses and chariots of fire round about Elisha.'' I do not know how any man can read the history of those times without admitting that the contest was decided by the upper forces.

My faith is in the upper forces, the upper armies. God is not dead! The chariots are not unwheeled. If you would only pray more and rub your eyes from the sleep of indifference and wash them in the cool, bright water fresh from the well of Christian reform, it would be said of you as it was said of old, ''the mountain was full of horses and chariots of fire round about Elisha.''

WOMAN

What is a Woman?—I have heard men tell in public places what a man is; but what is a woman? Until some one shall give a better definition I will tell you what a woman is. Direct from God a sacred and delicate gift with affections so great that no measuring line short of that of the infinite God can tell their bound. Fashioned to refine and soothe and elevate and irradiate home and society and the world. Of such value that no one can appreciate it, unless his mother lived long enough to let him understand it, or who, in some great crisis of life, when all else failed him, had a wife to reinforce him with a faith in God that nothing could disturb. Speak out, ye cradles, and tell of the feet that rocked you and the anxious faces that hovered over you! Speak out ye nurseries of all Christendom, and ye homes, whether desolate or still in full bloom with the faces of wife, mother and daughter, and help me to define what woman is. If a man during all his life accomplishes nothing else except to win the love and help and companionship of a good woman, he is the garlanded victor, and ought to have the hand of all people between here and the grave stretched out to him in congratulation. But as the geographers tell us that the depth of the sea corresponds with the heights of the mountains, I have to tell you that the good womanhood is not higher up than the bad womanhood is deep down.

Self-reliant Women.—Woman is a mere adjunct to men, an appendix to the masculine volume, an appendage, a sort of after-thought, something thrown in to make things even—that is the heresy entertained and implied by some men. This is evident to them: Woman's insignificance as compared to man is evident to them because Adam was first created and then Eve. They do not read the whole story or they would find that porpoise and the bear and the hawk were created before Adam, so that the argument drawn from priority of creation might prove that the sheep and the dog were greater than man. No, woman was an independent creation, and was intended, if she chose, to live alone, to walk alone, act alone, think alone, and fight the battle of life alone. The Bible says it is not good for man to live alone, but never says it is not good for woman to be alone, and the simple fact is that many women who are harnessed for life in the marriage relation would be a thousandfold better off if they were alone. God makes no mistake, and the fact that there is such a large majority of women in this land proves he intended that multitudes of them should go alone.

Ambitious Woman.—Oh, woman, is your wifely ambition noble or ignoble? Is it a high social position? That will then probably direct your husband, and he will climb and scramble and slip and fall and rise and tumble and on what level in what depth or height he will after while be found I cannot guess.

The contest for social position is the most unsatisfactory contest in all the world, because it is so uncertain about getting it, and so insecure a position after you have obtained it, and so unsatisfactory even if you keep it. The whisk of a lady's fan may blow it out; the growl of one bear or the bellowing of one bull on Wall Street scatter it.

Is the wife's ambition the political preferment of her husband? Then that will probably direct him. Many a wife has not been satisfied till her husband went into politics, but afterward would have given all she possessed to get him out.

Some of us could tell of what influence upon us has been a wifely ambition consecrated to righteousness. I have often been called of God, as I thought to run into the teeth of public opinion, and all outsiders with whom I advised told me I had better not, it would ruin me, my church. But in my home there has always been one voice to say: "Go ahead, and diverge not an inch from the straight line. Who cares if only God is on our side?" And although sometimes it seemed as if I was going out against 900 chariots, I went ahead, cheered by the domestic voice. A man is no better than his wife will let him be. O, wives of America, sway your scepters of influence for God and good homes.

Self-support.—When young women shall make up their minds at the start that masculine companionship is not a necessity in order to happiness and that there is a strong probability that they will have to fight the battle of life alone, they will be getting timber ready for their fortunes, and their saw and ax and plane sharpened for its construction since "every wise woman buildeth her house."

As no boy ought to be brought up without learning some business at which he could earn a livelihood, so no girl ought to be brought up without learning the science of self-support. The difficulty is that many a family goes sailing on the high tides of success, and the husband and father depends on his health and acumen for the welfare of his household; but one day he gets his feet wet, and in three days pneumonia has closed his life, and the daughters are turned out on a cold world to earn bread and there is nothing practical that they can do. How is this to be cured? Start clear back in the homestead and teach your daughters that life is an earnest thing and that there is a possibility, if not a probability that they will have to fight the battle of life alone. Let every father and mother say to their daughters, ''Now what would you do for a livelihood if what I now own were swept away by financial disaster, or old age or death should suddenly end my career?''

My advice to all girls and all unmarried women, whether in affluent homes or in homes where most stringent economies are grinding, is to learn to do some kind of work that the world must have while the world stands.

Bible on Woman's Attire.—God thought womanly attire of enough importance to have it discussed in the Bible. Paul, the apostle, by no means a sentimentalist, and accustomed to dwell on the great themes of God and the resurrection, writes about the arrangement of woman's hair and the style of her jewelry; Moses, his ear yet filled with the thunder at Mount Sinai, declares that womanly attire must be in marked contrast with masculine attire, and infraction of that law excites the indignation of high heaven. Just in proportion as the morals of a country or an age are depressed is that law defied. Show me the fashion plates of any century from the time of the Deluge to this, and I will tell you the exact state of public morals.

Personal Charms.—It would be sheer hypocrisy, because we may not have personal charms ourselves, to despise or affect to despise beauty in others. When God gives it, he gives it as a blessing and as a means of usefulness. David and his army were coming down from the mountains to destroy Nabal and his flocks and vineyards. The beautiful Abigail, the wife of Nabal, went out to arrest him when he came down from the mountains and she succeeded. Coming to the foot of the hill, she knelt. David with his army of sworn men came down over the cliffs, and when he saw her kneeling at the foot of the hill, he cried, "Halt! Halt!" That one beautiful woman kneeling at the foot of the cliff had arrested all those armed troops. A dewdrop dashed back Niagara. The Bible sets before us the portraits of Sarah and Rebecca and Abishag and Job's daughter, and says: "They were fair to look upon." By outdoor exercise and by skillful arrangement of apparel, let women make themselves attractive. The sloven has only one mission, and that is to excite our loathing and disgust. But alas for those who depend upon personal charms for their happiness! Beauty is such a subtle thing, it does not seem to depend upon facial proportions or upon the sparkle of the eye or upon the flush of the cheek. You sometimes find it among irregular features. It is the soul shining through the face that makes one beautiful.

No Happiness for Idle Women.—There is no happiness for an idle woman. It may be with hand, it may be with brain, it may be with foot; but work she must, or be wretched forever. The little girls of our families must be started with that idea. The curse of our American society is that our young women are taught that the first, second, third, fourth, fifth, sixth, seventh, tenth, fiftieth, thousandth thing in their life is to get somebody to take

care of them. Instead of that the first lesson should
be, how under God, they may take care of themselves. The simple fact is that a majority of them
do have to take care of themselves and that, too,
after having, through the false notions of their
parents, wasted the years in which they ought to
have learned how successfully to maintain themselves. We now and here declare the inhumanity,
cruelty and outrage of that father and mother who
pass their daughters into womanhood, having given
them no facility for earning their livelihood.
Madame de Stael said: "It is not these writings that
I am proud of, but the fact that I have facility in
ten occupations in any one of which I could make a
livelihood."

Nobility of Her Christian Influence.—My subject
impresses me with the regal influence of woman.
When I see Eve with this powerful influence over
Adam and over the generations that have followed,
it suggests to me that great power all women have
for good or for evil. I have no sympathy, nor have
you with the hollow flatteries showered upon woman
from the platform and the stage. They mean nothing; they are accepted as nothing. Woman's nobility consists in the exercise of a Christian influence;
and then I see this powerful influence of Eve upon
her husband and upon the whole human race, I make
up my mind that the frail arm of woman can strike
a blow which will resound through the eternity down
among the dungeons or up among the thrones. I
am not now speaking of representative women—of
Eve, who ruined the race by one fruit-picking; of
Jael, who drove a spike through the head of Sisera,
the warrior; of Esther, who overcame royalty; of
Abigail, who stopped a host by her own beautiful
prowess; of Mary, who nursed the world's Saviour;
of Grandmother Lois, immortalized in her grandson

Timothy; of Charlotte Corday, who drove the dagger through the heart of the assassin of her lover; or of Marie Antoinette, who by one look from the balcony of her castle quieted a mob, her own scaffold the throne of forgiveness and womanly courage. I speak not of these extraordinary persons, but of those who, unambitious for political power, as wives and mothers and sisters and daughters, attend to the thousand sweet offices of home.

When at last we come to calculate the forces that decided the destiny of nations, it will be found that the mightiest and grandest influence came from home, where the wife cheered up despondency and fatigue and sorrow by her own sympathy, and the mother trained her child for heaven, starting the little feet on the path to the Celestial City; and the sisters by their gentleness refined the manners of the brother; and the daughters were diligent in their kindness to the aged, throwing wreaths of blessing on the road that leads father and mother down the steep of years.

Angel in War.—In our Civil War, men cast the cannon, men fashioned the musketry, men cried to the hosts, "Forward, march!", men hurled their battalions on the sharp edges of the enemy, crying, "Charge! Charge!", but woman scraped the lint, woman administered the cordials, woman watched by the dying couch, woman wept at the solitary burial, attended by herself and four men with a spade. We greeted the generals home with brass bands and triumphal arches and wild huzzas; but the story is too good to be written anywhere, save in the chronicles of heaven, of Mrs. Brady, who came down among the sick in the swamps of the Chickahominy; of Annie Ross, in the cooper-shop hospital; of Margaret Breckinridge, who came to men who had been for weeks with their wounds undressed—some of them frozen to the ground, and when she turned them over, those that had an arm left, waved it and filled the air with their "Hurrah!"; of Mrs. Hodge, who came from Chicago, with blankets and with pillows, until the men shouted, "Three cheers for the Christian Commission!" God bless the women sitting down to take the last message: "Tell my wife not to fret about me, but to meet me in heaven; tell her to train up the boys whom we have loved so well; tell her we shall meet again in the good land; tell her to bear my loss like the Christian wife of a Christian soldier"; and of Mrs. Shelton, into whose face the convalescent soldier looked and said: "Your grapes and cologne cured me." And so it was also through the war with Spain—women heroic on the field, braving death and wounds to reach the fallen, watching by their fever cots in the West Indian hospitals or on the troopships or in our smitten home camps. Men did their work with shot and shell and carbine and howitzer; women did their work with socks and slippers and bandages and warm drinks and Scripture texts and gentle strokings of the hot temples and stories of that land where they never have any pain. Men knelt down over the wounded and said, "On which side did you fight?" Women knelt down over wounded and said, "Where are you hurt? What nice thing can I make for you to eat? What makes you cry?" To-night, while we men are sound asleep in our beds, there will be a light in yonder loft; there will be groaning down that dark alley; there will be cries of distress in that cellar. Men will sleep, and women will watch.

Make Yourself Worth While.—O young women of America, as many of you will have to fight your own battles, do not wait until you are flung by disaster upon the world; until your father is dead, and all the resources of your family have been scattered, but now while in good house and environment, surrounded by all prosperities, learn how to do some kind of work that the world must have. Turn your attention from making of flimsy nothings to the manufacturing of important somethings. Connect your skill with the indispensables of life. The world will always want something to wear, and something to eat, and shelter and fuel for the body, and knowledge for the mind, and religion for the soul. And all these things will continue to be the necessities, and if you fasten your energies upon occupations and professions thus related, the world will be unable to do without you. Remember that in proportion as you are skillful in anything your rivalries become less. For unskilled toil, women by the million. But you may rise to where there are only a thousand; and still higher till there are only a hundred; and still higher until there are only ten; and still higher in some particular department till there is only a unit and yourself. For a while you may keep wages and a place through the kindly sympathies of an employer, but you will eventually get no more compensation than you can make yourself worth.

Fighting the Battle of Life Alone.—Let me cheer all women fighting the battle of life alone with the fact that thousands of women have in that way won the day. Mary Lyon, founder of Mount Holyoke Female Seminary, fought the battle alone; Fidelia Fisk, the consecrated missionary, alone; Dorothea Dix, the angel of the insane asylum, alone; Caroline Herschel, the indispensable reinforcement of her brother, alone; Marie Takrzewska, the heroine of the Berlin hospital, alone; Helen Chalmers, patron of sewing-schools for the poor of Edinburgh, alone. And thousands and tens of thousands of women, of whose bravery and self-sacrifice and glory of character the world has made no record, but whose deeds are in the heavenly archives of martyrs who fought the battle alone, and, though unrecognized for the short fifty or eighty years of their earthly existence, shall through the quintillion ages of the higher world be pointed out with the admiring cry: "These are they who came out of great tribulation and had their robes washed and made white in the blood of the Lamb." The daughter of a regiment in any army is all surrounded by bayonets of defense, and in the battle whoever falls, she is kept safe. And you are the daughter of the regiment commanded by the Lord of Hosts. After all, you are not fighting the battle of life alone. All heaven is on your side.

Subject of Woman's Toil.—Society is to be re-instructed on the subject of woman's toil. A vast majority would have woman shut up to a few kinds of work. My judgment in this matter is, that a woman has a right to do anything she can do well. There should be no department of merchandise, mechanism, art, or science barred against her. If Miss Hosmer has genius for sculpture, give her a chisel. If Rosa Bonheur has a fondness for delineating animals, let her make "The Horse Fair." If Miss Mitchell will study astronomy, let her mount the starry ladder. If Lydia will be a merchant, let her sell purple. If Lucretia Mott will preach the Gospel, let her thrill with her womanly eloquence the audience in the Quaker meeting-house.

Queen of Home.—Solomon, by one stroke, set forth the imperial character of a true Christian woman. She is not a slave, not a hireling, not a subordinate, but a queen. Crown and courtly attendants and imperial wardrobe are not necessary to make a queen; but graces of the heart and life will give coronation to any woman. Woman's position is higher in the world than man's and although she has often been denied the right of suffrage, she always did vote and always will vote by her influence, and her chief desire ought to be that she should have grace rightly to rule in the dominion which she has already won.

Woman 1796-1782-1812.—A celebrated Frenchman by the name of Volney visited this country in 1796, and says of woman's diet in those times: "If a premium was offered for a regimen most destructive to health, none could be devised more efficacious for these ends than that in use among these people." That eclipses our lobster salad at midnight. Everybody talks about the dissipations of modern society and how womanly health goes down under it, but it was worse a hundred years ago, for the chaplain of a French regiment in our Revolutionary War wrote in 1782, in his book of American women, saying: "They are tall and well-proportioned, their features are generally regular, their complexions are generally fair and without color. At twenty years of age the women have no longer the freshness of youth. At thirty or forty they are decrepit." In 1812 a foreign consul wrote a book, entitled, "A Sketch of the United States at the Commencement of the Present Century," and he says of the women of those times: "At the age of thirty all their charms have disappeared." One glance at the portraits of the women a hundred years ago and their style of dress makes us wonder how they ever got their breath. All this makes me think that the express rail-train is no more an improvement on the old canal-boat, or the telegraph no more an improvement on the old-time saddlebags, than the women of our day are an improvement on the women of the last century.

Man's Inspiration.—No one can so inspire a man to noble purposes as a noble woman, and no one so thoroughly degrade a man as a wife of unworthy tendencies. While in the case of Jezebel we have an illustration of wifely ambition employed in the wrong direction, society and history are full of instances of wifely ambition gloriously triumphant in the right direction.

All that was worth admiration in the character of Henry VI was a reflection of the heroics of his wife Margaret. Justinian, the Roman emperor, confesses that his wise laws were the suggestions of his wife Theodora. Andrew Jackson, the warrior and President had his mightiest reënforcement in his plain wife, whose inartistic attire was the amusement of the elegant circles in which she was invited. Washington, who broke the chain that held America in foreign vassalage, wore for forty years a chain around his own neck, that chain holding the miniature likeness of her who had been his greatest inspiration, whether among the snows of Valley Forge or amid the honors of the presidential chair. Pliny's pen was driven through all its poetic and historical dominions by his wife. Pericles said he got all his eloquence and statesmanship from his wife.

De Tocqueville, whose writings will be potential and quoted while the world lasts, ascribes his successes to his wife, and says: "Of all the blessings which God has given me, the greatest of all in my eyes is to have lighted on Maria Motley." Martin Luther says of his wife: "I would not exchange my poverty with her and all the riches of Crœsus without her." Isabella, of Spain, by her superior faith in Columbus, put into the hand of Ferdinand, her husband, America.

John Adams, president of the United States, said of his wife: "She never, by word or look, discouraged me from running all the hazards for the salvation of my country's liberties.''

Thomas Carlisle spent the last years of his life in trying by his pen to atone for the fact that during his wife's life he never appreciated her influence on his career and destiny. The literary giant woke from his conjugal injustice and wrote the lamentations of Craigen-puttock and Chyne Row. A whole Greenwood of monumental inscriptions will not do a wife as much good as one plain sentence like that which Tom Hood wrote to his living wife when he said, ''I never was anything until I knew you.''

WORLD

A Changing World.—This world has been in process of change ever since it was created. Mountains born, mountains dying, and they have both cradle and grave. Once this planet was fluid, and no being such as you and I have ever seen, could have lived on it a minute. Our hemisphere turns its face to the sun, and then turns it back. The axis of the earth's revolution has shifted. The earth's center of gravity is changed. Once flowers grew in the Arctic and there was snow in the Tropics. There has been a re-distribution of land and sea, the land crumbling into the sea, the sea swallowing the land. Ice and fire have fought for the possession of this planet. The chemical composition of the air is different now from what it once was. Volcanoes once terribly alive are dead, not one throb of fiery pulse, not one breath of vapor. The ocean changing its amount of saline qualities. The internal fires of the earth are gradually eating their way to the surface. Upheaval and subsidence of vast helms of continent.

The changes of inanimate earth only symbolize the moral changes. Society ever becomes different, for better or worse. Boundary lines between nations are settled until the next war unsettles them. Uncertainty strikes through laws and customs and legislation. The characteristic of this world is that nothing in it is settled. At a time when we hoped that the arbitration planned last summer at The Hague, Holland would forever sheathe the sword and spike the gun and dismantle the fortress, the world has on hand two wars which are digging graves for the flower of English and American soldiery. From the presence of such geological and social and national and international unrest we turn with thanksgiving and exultation to find that there are things forever settled, but in higher latitudes than we have ever trod. "Forever, O Lord, thy word is settled in heaven." High up in the palace of the sun at least five things are settled: that nations which go continually and persistently wrong, perish; that happiness is the result of spiritual condition and not earthly environment; that this world is a schoolhouse for splendid or disgraceful graduation; that with or without us the world is to be made over into a scene of arborescence and purity; that all who are adjoined to the unparalleled One of Bethlehem and Nazareth and Golgotha will be the subjects of a supernal felicity without any taking off.

Do you doubt my first proposition, that nations which go wrong perish? We have in this American nation all the elements of permanence and destruction. We need not borrow from others any trowels for upbuildings or torches for demolition. Elements of ruin: Nihilism, and infidelity, agnosticism, Sabbath desecration, inebriety, sensuality, extravagance, fraud. They are all here. Elements of safety: God-worshiping men and women by scores of millions, honesty, benevolence, truthfulness, self-sacrifice, industry, sobriety, and more religion than has characterized any nation that has ever existed. They are all here. The only question is as to which forces will gain dominancy. The one class ascendant, and the United States Government I think will continue as long as the world exists. The other class ascendant and the United States goes into such small pieces that other governments would hardly think them worth picking up.

Our own nation will be judged by the same moral laws by which all other nations have been judged. The judgment day for individuals will probably come far on in the future. Judgment for nations is every day. Every day weighed, every day approved or every day condemned. Never before in the history of this country has the American nation been more surely in the balances than it is this minute. Do right and we go up. Do wrong and we go down. I am not so anxious to know what this statesman or that warrior thinks we had better do with Cuba and Puerto Rico and the Philippines as I am anxious to know what God thinks we ought to do. The destiny of this nation will not be decided on yonder Capitoline hill or at Manila or at the presidential ballot-box, for it will be settled in heaven.

Another thing decided in the same place is that happiness is the result of spiritual condition not of earthly environment. Sometimes happiness is seated on a footstool and sometimes misery on a throne. All the gold of earth in one chunk cannot purchase five minutes of complete satisfaction. Worldly success is an atmosphere that breeds the maggots of envy and jealousy and hate. There are those who will never forgive you if you have more emoluments or honor or ease than they have. Your heaven is their hell.

A dying president of the United States said many years ago, in regard to his lifetime of experience, "It don't pay." The leading statesmen of America, in letters of advice, warn young men to keep out of politics. Many of the most successful have tried in vain to drown their troubles in strong drink. On the other hand there are millions of people who on departing this life will have nothing to leave but a good name and a life insurance, their illumined faces are indices of illumined souls. There is so much heartiness and freedom from care in their laughter that when you hear it you are compelled to laugh in sympathy, although you know not what they are laughing about.

Another thing decided in that high place is that this world is a schoolhouse or college for splendid or disgraceful graduation. We begin in the freshman class of good or evil and then pass into the sophomore, and then into the junior, and then into the senior, and from that we graduate angels or devils. In many colleges there is an "elective course," where the student selects what he will study—mathematics, or the languages or chemistry, or philosophy; and it is an elective course we all take in the schoolhouse or university of this world.

We may study sin until we are saturated with it, or righteousness until we are exemplifications of it. Graduate we must, but we decide for ourselves the style of graduation. It is an elective course. We can study generosity until our every word and every act and every contribution of money or time will make the world better or we may study meanness until our soul shall shrink up to a smallness unimaginable. We may educate ourselves into an irascibility that will ever and anon keep our face flushed with wrath and every nerve aquiver. Great schoolhouse of a world, in which we are all being educated for glory or perdition.

Some have wondered why graduation day in college is called "commencement day" when it is the last day of college exercises, but graduation days are properly called commencement days. To all graduates it is the commencement of active life, and our graduation day from earth will be to us commencement of our chief life, our larger life, our tremendous life, our eternal life. What a mighty day it will be when we graduate from this world! Will it be hisses of condemnation or handclapping of approval? Will there be flung to us nettles or wreaths? Will it be a resounding "Come" or a reverberating "Depart"?

In the real college before graduation and commencement comes examination day, and before our graduation and commencement will come examination. It will be asked what we have been doing, what we have learned under the tutelage of years of joy and sorrow and under the teaching of the Holy Ghost are we educated for heaven. Have we done our best with the curriculum of study put before every mortal and immortal? Oh, this world is a schoolhouse for splendid or disgraceful graduation and death is commencement. All that is settled in heaven.

A Stage.—Each one of us is put on the stage of this world to take some part. You and I are expected to take some especial particular part in the great human immortal life. Through what hardship and suffering and discipline artists went through year after year that they might be perfected in their parts, you have often read. We are put on the stage of this life to represent charity, and faith, and humility, and helpfulness—what little preparation we have made, although we have three galleries of spectators—earth and heaven and hell! Have we not been more attentive to the part taken by others than to the part taken by ourselves, and while we needed to be looking at home and concentrating on our duty, we have been criticising the other performers, and saying "that was too high" or "too low" or "too feeble" or "too extravagant" or "too tame" or "too demonstrative," while we were making ourselves a dead failure and preparing to be ignominiously hissed off the stage?

Each one is assigned a place, no supernumeraries hanging around the drama of life to take this or that or the other part. *No one can take our place.* We can take no other place. Ay, it is not the impersonation of another; we ourselves are the real Merchant of Venice, or the real filial Cordelia or the real cruel Regan; the real Portia or the real Lady Macbeth. The tragedian of the playhouse at the close of the third scene of the fifth act, takes off the attire of Gonzalo or Edward Mortimer or Henry V, and resigns the character in which for three hours he appeared. But we never put off our character, and no change of apparel can make us any one else than that which we eternally are.

Many make a failure of their part in the drama of life. The world cheers before it damns. So it is said, the deadly asp tickles before it stings. Going up is he? Hurrah! Hurrah! Stand back and let his galloping horses dash by a whirlwind of plated harness and tinkling headgear and arched neck. Drink deep of his prosperity. *Going down* is he? Pretend that you cannot see him as he passes. When men ask you if you know him, halt and hesitate. Applause when he went up. Sibilant derision when he came down. "Men shall clap their hands at him and hiss him out of his place."